The Black Arch

THE CURSE
OF FENRIC

By Una McCormack

Published September 2018 by Obverse Books

Cover Design © Cody Schell

Text © Una McCormack, 2018

Range Editors: Paul Simpson, Philip Purser-Hallard

Dedication

My thanks and love as ever to Matthew, for helping me through this project.

CONTENTS

OVERVIEW

Serial Title: *The Curse of Fenric*

Writer: Ian Briggs

Director: Nicholas Mallett

Original UK Transmission Dates: 25 October 1989 – 15 November 1989

Running Time: Episode 1: 24m 23s

                       Episode 2: 24m 09s

                       Episode 3: 24m 11s

                       Episode 4: 24m 16s

UK Viewing Figures: Episode 1: 4.3 million

                       Episode 2: 4.0 million

                       Episode 3: 4.0 million

                       Episode 4: 4.2 million

Regular Cast: Sylvester McCoy (The Doctor), Sophie Aldred (Ace)

Guest Cast: Dinsdale Landen (Dr Judson), Alfred Lynch (Commander Millington), Tomek Bork (Captain Sorin), Nicholas Parsons (Reverend Wainwright), Janet Henfrey (Miss Hardaker), Joan Kenney (Jean), Joanne Bell (Phyllis), Anne Reid (Nurse Crane), Raymond Trickett (Ancient One)

Antagonists: Fenric

Novelisation: *Doctor Who: The Curse of Fenric* by Ian Briggs. **The Target Doctor Who Library** #151.

Sequels: 'Games' {short story, 1992), 'Ace of Hearts' (short story, 1998), *Night Thoughts* (audio, 2006), *Casualties of War* (audio, 2008), *Black and White* (audio, 2012), *Gods and Monsters* (audio, 2012), *The Wolves of Winter* (comic, 2017)

Responses:

'What is abundantly clear is that the series in its death throes wasn't going down without a fight. A very commendable fight it was, too.'

[Mark Braxton, *Radio Times Online*]

'It's not the best episode for the uninitiated, and the dialogue can be a little pretentious, but none of that really matters. This is a wonderful, emotional, frightening, gripping episode with more thematic richness than just about any other episode of **Doctor Who**.'

[Carson Maynard, *From A to 7Q*]

SYNOPSIS

Episode 1

The Doctor and **Ace** arrive at a naval base in 1940s England, where the Doctor is able to bluff his way into a meeting with **Doctor Judson**, the wheelchair-bound creator of a revolutionary code-breaking computer, ULTIMA.

On a nearby beach, a group of Soviet soldiers under the leadership of **Captain Sorin** make a landing. One of their two dinghies disappears in the fog, with only a sole, apparently insane, survivor making it to shore. Sorin sends one of the other soldiers to retrieve a set of sealed orders which had been on the second dinghy. He finds them and sees that they contain a photograph of Judson. Before he can return them to Sorin, however, he is killed by something from the sea.

At the local church the next day, the Doctor talks to the vicar, **Reverend Wainwright**, who mentions a curse, and Judson, who is copying Viking runes. Meanwhile Ace befriends two London evacuees, **Jean** and **Phyllis**.

Ace meets the two teenagers later, close to the spot at which the Soviets landed. The Doctor finds the Soviet orders and hurries back to the church, telling Ace not to go in the water. She follows his instructions, but falls out with Jean and Phyllis when they go swimming.

At the church, Wainwright shows the Doctor a translation of the Viking runes in which Judson is so interested. He recognises similarities between the translation and the Soviet orders. Ace returns, having abandoned her two new friends to their swimming, and is outraged by the behaviour of the base commander, **Commander Millington**, when he threatens to dismiss one young radio operator, **Kathleen Dudman**, for bringing her baby daughter to work with her.

The Doctor and Ace discover that Millington's office is an exact replica of a cipher room in Berlin – Millington hopes to understand how the Germans think. However, the Doctor also notices an old school cricket photo which demonstrates that Millington and Judson knew one another before the war – and a chess set.

Back at the beach, the Doctor and Ace discover the body of the dead Soviet soldier. As the Doctor examines the corpse, the other soldiers surround them.

Episode 2

Quoting from the sealed orders they have just discovered help the Doctor and Ace convince the soldiers to take them to Sorin. After the Doctor calms the survivor of the lost dinghy enough for him to hand over a strangely shaped metallic object, Sorin allows them to leave unscathed.

Returning to the church, the Doctor discovers a new set of Viking runes burned into the crypt wall. He searches for a secret passageway but is found by Millington, who reveals a hidden chamber in which the British are working on a toxin to use against the Nazis. Again, the Doctor is able to convince his captor that they are on the same side, and Millington agrees to tell him everything, though he orders Ace to leave first. She speaks to Rev. Wainwright, who confesses the war has had a negative impact on his faith.

Millington tells the Doctor that the poor security on the base is a deliberate ploy, designed to lure in the Soviets, who he knows intend to steal the ULTIMA machine. What they do not know, however, is that Millington has secreted a bomb in the machine's heart, which will explode on the transmission of a code word. Millington demonstrates the effects of the toxin on a cage of doves at the same time as a troop of British soldiers are killed on the beach by the Soviets. One Soviet soldier, walking alone on the beach, sees Jean and Phyllis in the water and, lured in by them, is attacked and killed.

Millington obsessively draws images of flasks, unaware that his men have found – and discarded - just such a flask at the church. Judson translates the runic inscription as 'Let the Chains of Fenric shatter' but Ace points out it could also be a logic code capable of being run into the ULTIMA machine. Judson rushes off to do so.

The Doctor and Ace go to warn Jean and Phyllis of the danger in the water but, at the cottage at which they are staying, they find **Miss Hardaker**, the lady on whom they are billeted, murdered and drained of blood. Running back to the church they are just in time to save the vicar from the vampiric Jean and Phyllis. The Doctor assures everyone that all will be well so long as Judson does not realise that the Viking runes are a computer program – exactly what Ace had told him!

The Doctor tries to stop Judson, but is too late. The computer is printing off the names of the original Viking settlers – and vampires are simultaneously rising from the waves and moving inland.

Episode 3

Millington intends to protect the ULTIMA machine until the program completes, but the deliberately weak security at the base makes this difficult. The Doctor reveals that **Haemovores**, vampiric entities from the far future, are on their way to the base. Ace goes to check on Kathleen Dudmore and her baby and finds them packing to leave, while the Doctor attempts to identify the descendants of the original Vikings. Hoping to help the Doctor, Ace goes to the church and picks up the flask.

Sorin and his men have followed the Haemovores and arrive at the church just in time to save Ace from an attack by two of them, but they – and the Doctor and Wainwright – are forced to take sanctuary in the vestry. The Doctor explains that faith is the only weapon effective against the Haemovores. He uses his own faith in his companions to force the creatures back, and Sorin uses his faith in the Soviet revolution to drive a path through them, allowing all but two of the Soviets to return to the beach. The Doctor, Ace and Wainwright escape to the base but Millington confiscates the flask and locks the remaining Soviet soldiers in with the Haemovores.

Sorin fails in an attempt to join forces with Millington against the Haemovores, and is instead imprisoned by the British. Millington inserts the flask in the ULTIMA machine, and explains that he blames himself for Judson's injuries and had promised him supreme power which he will achieve through the power of Fenric. After Kathleen tells Ace that her husband **Frank** has been killed in action, Ace confronts the Doctor, who admits that the flask contains an ancient evil on the verge of breaking free.

Ace and the Doctor combine to free Sorin, and they attempt to recover the flask, but are too late. Led by Jean and Phyllis, the Haemovores break into the base. Wainwright attempts to use his flagging religious faith to stop them but is unsuccessful. The program fed into the ULTIMA machine concludes and the flask blasts all of its power in to Judson. As the Doctor, Ace and Sorin arrive Judson is standing on his feet, waiting for the Doctor...

Episode 4

Judson, now possessed by Fenric, disappears and in the aftermath Millington orders **Captain Bates** to execute the Doctor and his companions by firing squad for treason. Fortunately, Sorin's troops intervene and the Doctor and his friends are able to escape. In need of a chess set so that the Doctor can complete his game with Fenric, they attempt to take Millington's from his office, but it has been booby-trapped and they are almost killed. Instead, they take a set from Kathleen Dudman's suitcase and while Ace stays with Kathleen, the Doctor lays a trap for Fenric. The vampiric Jean and Phyllis summon the **Ancient One**, eldest of the Haemovores, to come to meet Fenric.

After the British soldiers win their fight with the Soviets, the Haemovores kill them. Bates overhears Judson/Fenric telling Millington that the Haemovores will use the toxins stored at the base to poison all of Earth's oceans. Bates forms an alliance with Sorin and the one remaining Soviet soldier, **Vershinin**, to fight Fenric and his allies.

Ace helps Kathleen Dudman escape both the Haemovores and the base, and is then shocked as Jean and Phyllis and the other Haemovores disintegrate on Fenric's orders. Fenric is engaged in attempting to solve the Doctor's chess puzzle and while he is distracted, the Doctor tells the Ancient One that fulfilling Fenric's plan will simply set in motion events which lead to the polluted Earth from which the Haemovores have come.

In a shootout, Millington is killed by a combination of Vershinin and Bates. This unlikely alliance prompts Ace to recognise the solution to the Doctor's chess puzzle. When she discovers Sorin standing over Judson's body, she tells him the solution – only to discover that Sorin is dead, and Fenric has taken over his body.

Fenric makes the winning move, and then tells Ace that Kathleen is her grandmother and her baby the mother Ace despises, **Audrey**. Millington, Wainwright, Judson – even Ace – all were pawns in Fenric's chess game against the Doctor. Confident in his victory, Fenric orders the Ancient One to kill the Doctor and Ace, but Ace's faith in the Doctor holds the creature back, until the Doctor callously tells Fenric that he does not care if Ace is killed; he has known all along that she was nothing more than a pawn. Her faith in the Doctor shaken, Ace can no longer hold back the Ancient One. He steps forward and, remembering the Doctor's words about the Earth's future, destroys both Fenric and himself.

The Doctor apologises for his callous claims about Ace, and explains that he had to destroy her faith in him for his plan to work. Ace goes swimming off the beach, with much on her mind...

INTRODUCTION

Let us pause the DVD for the moment and consider two fixed points in time.

The evening of Wednesday 8 November 1989: episode 3 of *The Curse of Fenric* is transmitted. 'We play the contest again, Time Lord,' Fenric says, rising from Judson's wheelchair to challenge the Doctor to another round in a battle that has taken place again and again throughout space and time.

The night of Thursday 9 November, 1989: after an announcement during the day that border regulations were to be relaxed, crowds of East Berliners begin gathering at the Berlin Wall, demanding permission to cross into West Germany. Around 10:45pm, the commander of the Bornholmer Straße border crossing allowed the guards to open the checkpoints and let people through with little or no identity checking. A little later that night, both East and West Germans began to chip away at the Wall, beginning the process of its demolition.

Correlation is by no means causation, and the storm of history continues unabated, racking up more devastation in its wake. We seem a long way from this time now. But these two moments encapsulate what I intend to be the central impulses of this short book: that contemporary culture arises from a zeitgeist, and that by looking at, considering, and close reading *The Curse of Fenric*, we can both revisit a moment in British social, cultural, and political life, and, secondly, use that moment to understand the processes underway that bring us to the present moment. Where the future goes is anyone's guess. All that we can do is consider the uses to which we put history: what we choose to foreground, what we choose to occlude; which narratives we push forwards, which we try to repress.

For this author, *The Curse of Fenric* is the best story in what was, at that point, the best season yet of **Doctor Who**. In other words, I love it. More than any other story, it shows me what **Doctor Who** can do. You will love other stories better, and you'll have your reasons. They're probably good reasons too, and they might even persuade me, for the moment. But when I think about *The Curse of Fenric*, I am somewhat in awe. There's great confidence in the story-telling, and great courage too, given the institutional context at the time. The performances are joyful, moving, surprising. The 'message' (of which more later) presses all my buttons. If you caught me in the moment and asked me to name my favourite story, this is the one I would say (before equivocating and adding, 'Well, of course, and *The Caves of Androzani* [1984] and *Gridlock* [2007]...').

Let me tell you what I'm going to do.

Throughout this long essay I position *The Curse of Fenric* as a pivotal moment in the unfolding text of **Doctor Who**. The chapters that follow examine the text (or versions of the text, since there are several) to allow me to consider several trends in the show's history which emerge distinctively for the first time around this time. These include familiar points about serialisation, the increasing prominence and psychological complexity of the companion (with the concomitant shift to emotionally-driven story arcs), and the story's role (through its novelisation and numerous 'versions') in expanding the transmedia storytelling that leads to the proliferation of ancillary texts that exist around the show today.

In **Chapter 1,** I consider the story as part of a broader response to Thatcherism both within the BBC and beyond. In **Chapter 2**, I reflect upon the story's unique position as the only 'classic' story with a setting during the Second World War and consider how the setting is handled in comparison to the post-2005 stories with a similar setting. In **Chapter 3**, I discuss the women in the story as part of a wider analysis of women in science fiction. And in **Chapter 4**, I examine how the story is part of a reconfiguration of the Doctor's mythic identity away from a hero of reason and technocracy to a champion of what I call mythic or secular humanism.

Another moment from 1989: the American political scientist Francis Fukuyama publishes an influential essay, 'The End of History?', in which he argues that Western liberal democracy was now so dominant and ubiquitous that:

> 'What we may be witnessing is not just the end of the Cold War, or the passing of a particular period of post-war history, but the end of history as such: that is, the end point of mankind's ideological evolution and the universalisation of Western liberal democracy as the final form of human government.'[1]

There was to be no alternative, no progression, beyond liberal democracy.

A few years later, in 1992, Fukuyama expanded his history into a full-length book, *The End of History and the Last Man*. I read this book around this time at university and I was not convinced. In 1989, *The Curse of Fenric* was not convinced by this kind of argument either. In 2018, it seems woefully naïve. If there is an underlying theme to this

---

[1] Fukuyama, Francis, 'The End of History?' *The National Interest* #16, Summer 1989.

book, it is the writing of history, and the uses that we make of history. The contest, it seems, happens again and again, a war without end.

CHAPTER 1: DOCTOR WHO vs TINA

Fucking Thatcher

During the 1980s, the British public was often reminded by the Conservative government (and its own Helen A) that 'There Is No Alternative' (or 'TINA'). By this was meant that the market economy, free trade, and globalised capitalism were by far the best means of securing and distributing wealth and freedom, and that other models, in particular state socialism, had failed to deliver wealth, health, liberty, and the flourishing of the human spirit to their subjects. For British Prime Minister Margaret Thatcher, the idea went beyond the pragmatic notion that market forces were the most efficient way to organise; it arose from her basic moral imperative that human beings should be free to exercise choice. This principle lies behind the political project that we generally call 'Thatcherism': free trade, freedom of the market, entrepreneurialism, privatisation, etc. I'll leave critiques aside; you're either for or against. It's enough for my purposes here to note that the mainstream political rhetoric of the 1980s insisted that there was no alternative to market – an ideological stance predicated, paradoxically, upon giving people choice[2].

Certainly the rhetoric of the market was gaining ground at the BBC during this time. The organisation was undergoing the changes that would eventually result in Birtism and in the internal market. The

---

[2] 'You can have any colour you like,' Henry Ford is supposed to have said, 'as long as it's black.' Notice also that beyond the moral and political projects here there lies a conception of history as having reached an end-state, a 'best state', that is closely related to Fukuyama's 'End of History' thesis.

Peacock Committee was set up in 1985 to review the Corporation's funding; although the 1986 report did call for the outsourcing of a significant proportion of the BBC's output, it did not suggest the ending of the licence fee as the government had expected. After this, something of a coup d'état occurred at the BBC: pro-Thatcherite Marmaduke Hussey was appointed Chairman of the Board of the Governors in 1986; this led within three months to the forced resignation in 1987 of Director-General Alasdair Milne, who had repeatedly been in high-profile conflict with the Conservative government[3]. Milne's replacement, Michael Checkland, had a background in accountancy; his deputy, John Birt, would become his successor as Director-General in 1992. Under Birt's aegis the organisational reforms at the BBC would bring about a full-blown internal market, known, perhaps inevitably, as 'Producer Choice'[4].

Within this shifting and challenging context, **Doctor Who** had of course been having its own difficulties. The programme's high-profile hiatus in 1985 is well documented, as are the subsequent very public and vicious falling out between producer John Nathan-Turner and

---

[3] Leapman, Michael, 'Alasdair Milne: BBC Executive Who Rose to Director-General But Was Sacked under Pressure from Mrs Thatcher', *The Independent*, 10 January 2013.

[4] Producer Choice is an excellent study of the unintended consequences of bureaucratic reform. Intended to make the costs of programming transparent by making BBC departments charge each other for goods and services, it led to notorious absurdities such as researchers going out to buy CDs rather than using one of the best sound archives in the world. Not unintentionally, perhaps, it also led to the loss of 5,000 jobs. See Plunkett, John, 'BBC Puts an End to Producer Choice', *The Guardian*, 22 March 2006

script editor Eric Saward, and the summary sacking of Colin Baker[5]. By season 26, the programme had returned to a more even keel thanks to the combination of the highly experienced Nathan-Turner with a new, young script editor, Andrew Cartmel. This was Cartmel's first job in television; despite his lack of experience, he nonetheless had a clear idea of what he wanted to achieve. In particular, he was keen to bring back science fiction to a programme that had, to his mind, become bogged-down in tired thrillers, and, of course, he was set on restoring mystery to the figure of the Doctor.

Cartmel set about commissioning new writers with fresh ideas[6]. His diaries at the time give the impression almost of an open-door policy, like a prototype writers' room: during the production of *Dragonfire* (1987) he recalls having Ben Aaronovitch, Ian Briggs, and Stephen Wyatt in the room all at once: '[F]or the next quarter of an hour we had three of the best young writers in Britain trying to come up with a name for a futuristic fruit drink'[7]. Cartmel's policy continued throughout season 26. Ian Briggs recalls:

> 'Andrew facilitated a lot of interaction between us. We'd sometimes overlap script meetings if someone arrived early or overran, and chat about each other's story and scripts, sometimes offering ideas or feedback. Andrew also fed us updates on each other's scripts and gave us finished drafts. And he gave me finished drafts during my season off and

---

[5] Extensively documented in Marson, Richard, *JN-T: The Life and Scandalous Times of John Nathan-Turner.*
[6] Only Pip and Jane Baker had previously written for **Doctor Who**, and their story was a holdover from the previous season.
[7] Cartmel, Andrew, *Script Doctor: The Inside Story of Doctor Who 1986-89*, pp77-78.

introduced me to the new writers. Occasionally we dropped in one another's shoots. So we knew what was happening in each other's stories and could draw on them or support them, as in Ace's reference in *Fenric* to the old house in *Ghost Light* [1989].'[8]

To watch **Doctor Who** during this period is to see a narrative and production renaissance: there's great playfulness and quirkiness, particularly in earlier stories such as *Paradise Towers, Delta and the Bannermen* (both 1987), and *The Happiness Patrol* (1988). Increasingly there is a seriousness of intent. By the final season (by which time Cartmel had realised that period rather than futuristic settings played to the strengths of the designers), there is real ambition in the complexity of the stories being made. *The Curse of Fenric* and *Ghost Light* are the highpoint of this. Some of these experiments don't work; some point forwards to new forms of televisual storytelling.

The two opening episodes of *The Curse of Fenric*, for example, seem to hover between the straightforward storytelling of earlier, more theatrical television drama, and a speedier intercutting of scenes more reminiscent of film. This does sometimes affect the coherence of the story; the viewer has to adjust between the two modes, and try to understand whether scenes are happening immediately after each other, or with some time lapse between them. But the production is deeply ambitious, particularly given the schedule: the whole story is shot in 14 days between 3 April and 20 April 1989, a remarkable achievement for what is, in effect, a short film[9]. Notably,

---

[8] Personal communication with the author, April 2018.
[9] *Doctor Who: The Complete History* Volume 46, p75.

The Curse of Fenric is a period drama made entirely on location, five years before **Middlemarch** (1994), which is generally held to have revolutionised and refreshed BBC period drama. Of course, there are fewer vampires in George Eliot.

The tragedy is that the programme was at the time deeply unloved by the institution, considered tired, dated, and something of an embarrassment. Peter Cregeen, Head of Series at BBC Drama at the time, and rather gamely interviewed for the *Survival* DVD extra 'Endgame' (where he calls himself 'the man who cancelled **Doctor Who**'), states that the general feeling was that the show needed a rest. The story of **Doctor Who** between 1987 and 1989 is one of a slow smothering, with nobody willing to take the flak for cancelling the programme outright, while various parties conspired to ensure the impossibility of its continued existence. Scheduled against **Coronation Street** (1960-) and led by a producer who was desperate to leave[10], the odds were stacked against **Doctor Who** surviving into the 1990s. There was uncertainty during the transmission of *The Curse of Fenric* (and *Survival* (1989)[11]): on 23 October 1989 (two days before the first episode was transmitted) DJ Steve Wright stated on his BBC Radio 1 show that there would be no new series of the programme in 1990; on 1 November, the day of the broadcast of episode 2, Anne Robinson on **Points of View** denied the programme had been axed[12]. In early February 1990 it was revealed that contract options for Sylvester McCoy and Sophie Aldred had not been taken

---

[10] See Marson, *JN-T,* particularly chapter 12, 'Persuaded to Stay'.
[11] Cartmel's addition of the Doctor's last speech to the end of *Survival* makes it clear that the production team knew there wasn't going to be a show in the near future.
[12] *The Complete History* #46, p78-9.

up. John Nathan-Turner left the BBC in August 1990[13]. By the end of 1990, an announcement had been made that the show would not be produced in-house.

Given this institutional context, then, I find it remarkable that *The Curse of Fenric* exists. Not in the way that we are used to being delighted at the existence of episodes of **Doctor Who**, rescued from skips and furnaces, like Woody, Buzz and the gang at the end of *Toy Story 3*, but rather I am delighted that a story so fresh, complex, satisfying, and defiant was made under the conditions in which *The Curse of Fenric* was made. We are used, when telling the history of **Doctor Who**, of hearing of missing episodes retrieved from behind filing cabinets, or scraps of lost stories assembled from Australian cuts, etc. But with *The Curse of Fenric*, we have a story that not only exists in its entirety but exists in multiple forms. Unlike some **Doctor Who** stories from the 1960s, *The Curse of Fenric* is assembled not from fragmentary telesnaps, or from ghostly audio material summoning up the past like a Nigel Kneale play. Instead, we have a glut of material: the original broadcast, the edited video release, the recut 'film' for the DVD release, a novelisation, contemporaneous production notes, near-contemporaneous 'fan'-written production histories, anecdotes related at convention appearances... The text of *The Curse of Fenric* is inherently unstable: there was hesitancy over the finished form even during production, when a fifth episode was briefly mooted (there wasn't quite enough extra footage, but this material formed the basis for the two later cuts for the video and then the DVD release)[14].

---

[13] *The Complete History* #46, p122-3.
[14] *The Complete History* #46, p76.

The novelisation of *The Curse of Fenric*, released the year after transmission, tells us from the start to abandon any fixed notion of the text:

> 'Every story must have a beginning, a middle and an end. But it's never that simple [...] All the time, the Earth slowly turns, joining all the stories together – day after day, year upon year. They are joined into one long story with no beginning and no end. However far back you go, you can never find a first beginning. There's always something earlier.'[15]

Formally, too, the novelisation assembles its story not in linear fashion, but shifting between texts, asking us to assemble a version from ancillary material or 'Documents', such as a school essay showing Millington's childhood obsession with the Norse Gods and Ragnarok, a section of a Norse saga 'The Curse of the Flask', a letter from Bram Stoker to his wife that suggests that his novel *Dracula* was in part inspired by the curse, and an 'Arabian Tale' documenting a chess contest between Aboo-Fenran and El-Dok'Tar. These, plus the more fleshed out characters that appear in the book, expand the text of the story significantly. *The Curse of Fenric*, as much as any lost Troughton story, makes us abandon notions of canonicity, of a fixed text, and the numerous versions – visual and text – invited fans at the time to start to learn to consume television in a new way, one in which texts would be enlarged and expanded by ancillary material. We all watch television this way now. We didn't then[16]. The multiple

---

[15] Briggs, Ian, *Doctor Who: The Curse of Fenric*, p1.

[16] The novelisation was published in 1990. The video was released in 1991 with 6 minutes of extra material. A DVD release in 2003 included an edited 'movie-length' edition with new effects, and 12 minutes of new footage.

forms of *The Curse of Fenric* invite us to interpret the story over and over again; it is a story that never ends, one inherently full of alternatives. Formally, the book refutes TINA.

That the programme at this time was pursuing an anti-Thatcherite agenda has become part of the history, and certainly Cartmel, in the introduction to his memoir *Script Doctor*, based on his diaries written at the time, is at pains to make his anti-government credentials clear. In the introduction to the book, Sylvester McCoy recalls John Nathan-Turner telling him that:

> 'He interviewed Andrew and they were getting along well and then he sprang the crucial question. "If you could achieve one thing with **Doctor Who**, what would it be?" Andrew, without an instant's hesitation, replied "Overthrow the government"'.[17]

There is an element of self-mythologising about this, perhaps, but it was all sufficiently plausible to bring *The Daily Telegraph* out in hives well into the new millennium: 'Left-wing script writers infiltrated **Doctor Who** to give it anti-Thatcher plot lines in the late 1980s in a failed attempt "to overthrow the Government" Sylvester McCoy has claimed', the paper howled, in 2010[18]. The article goes on to paint a picture of the **Doctor Who** production team in the late 80s as exactly the kind of leftie luvvies that the right-wing press loves to hate. Cartmel, interviewed for the piece, is rather rueful about the outcome of his revolutionary efforts:

> 'Critics, media pundits and politicians certainly didn't pick up

---

[17] Cartmel, *Script Doctor*, p7.
[18] Adams, Stephen, '*Doctor Who* "Had Anti-Thatcher Agenda"'. The *Telegraph*, 14 February 2010

on what we were doing. If we had generated controversy and become a cause célèbre we would have got a few more viewers but, sadly, nobody really noticed or cared'[19].

There's something touching about *The Telegraph* catching up in 2010 with what was in plain sight in 1988. *The Happiness Patrol* contains, in Helen A, a caricature of the Prime Minister that makes her **Spitting Image** puppet appear flattering. Season 26 in general is thematically concerned with the Thatcherite shibboleth of competition, repeatedly offering stories and resolutions in which competitive activity is critiqued and cooperative behaviour wins the day[20]. *Battlefield* (1989) shows an ages-long conflict in which Morgaine is prepared to sacrifice her son rather than leave; the conflict is ended less through the Brigadier's defence of his planet in the face of the Destroyer than by the Doctor's appeal to Morgaine's reason and sense of honour. *Survival* deconstructs the prevailing Social Darwinism of the 1980s, showing competitive behaviour as leading to mutually assured destruction: 'If we fight like animals, we die like animals!' the Doctor cries, refusing to continue his conflict with the Master. Light's insistence in *Ghost Light* on wiping out life on Earth rather have his catalogue become invalid represents the irrational logic of totalitarianism, which prefers to kill rather than be proven wrong, and self-destructs in the face of the knowledge of evolution's uncontrollable growth and diversity (and the cooperation of Control, Fenn-Cooper, and Nimrod). In *The Curse of Fenric*, Fenric represents the apocalyptic ideologies of Nazism; the logic of war is shown to be corrupting most profoundly in Millington, who can only see enemies,

---

[19] Adams, Stephen, '*Doctor Who* "Had Anti-Thatcher Agenda"'. The *Telegraph,* 14 February 2010
[20] See my essay on this, 'No Competition', in *Chicks Unravel Time*.

and is already looking past the current war to the next one. War, for Millington, has become a state of mind, not a reasoned and limited response to threat, a habit of thought that will make the pre-emptive strike of sending a deadly poison to wipe out Moscow appear to be a rational act.

The resolution to all this conflict and competition, as given in *The Curse of Fenric*, is markedly political: the 'solution' that eludes Fenric is not a trick by the Doctor, or the continuance of warfare, but the refusal to play the game, by the pawns breaking ranks. In other words, the international solidarity of the proletariat. At the end of *The Curse of Fenric*, British Tommy and Soviet Comrade unite, refusing to continue the fight of their superiors. 'War,' says Vershinin, 'a game played by politicians'. (It's notable that, apart from the Doctor, Ace, and Ace's mother and grandmother, these are the only other characters to survive the story – or, if they do die, we don't see it on screen. In the novelisation, they are killed[21]. I exercise my rights as reader and thus co-creator of the text to choose to consider this non-canonical.) There is also the romantic union of Sorin (who has unshakeable belief in the principles of the Revolution) and Ace (the granddaughter of a man serving in the Merchant Navy). Sorin's gift to Ace of his hammer and sickle badge represents a promise of love and cooperation that transcends national ties, and the Cold War to come. (In the novelisation, Ace goes back in time to 1887 to marry the great-grandfather of Sorin, Count Sorin; it's not clear how they fare during the Revolution.)

In other ways, too, *The Curse of Fenric* is addressing the prevailing moral war cries of the right at the time, particularly the emphasis on

---

[21] Briggs, *The Curse of Fenric*, p178.

family values, within, naturally, heterosexual marriage. Targets for Conservative ire included single mothers, particularly those assumed to be getting pregnant to jump the housing queue, and gay men and women, legislated against in Section 28 of the 1988 Local Government Act. This stated that a local authority 'shall not intentionally promote homosexuality or publish material with the intention of promoting homosexuality' or 'promote the teaching in any maintained school of the acceptability of homosexuality as a pretended family relationship'. It led to the closure, self-censorship, or limitation of the activities of many LGBT support groups, was actively campaigned against from the outset, eventually repealed in 2000 in Scotland, and 2003 in the rest of the UK.

The Curse of Fenric, particularly in the novelisation, examines the deleterious effects of repressed desire and the denial of love: Millington's suppressed love for Judson, and his guilt over the accident which has crippled Judson, which Millington caused in a fit of jealousy seeing Judson 'smile across to one of the other players, a tall, blond boy with clear blue eyes and a strong body,'[22] is the means by which Fenric is able to use him. The point is less that Millington is gay, but that his unspoken and repressed desire is harmful. The codeword that Millington chooses to detonate the booby-trap within the Ultima Machine, waging chemical warfare on the Soviets, is 'Love'. The story too pushes back against prevailing Conservative rhetoric towards single mothers. Kathleen Dudman is deeply offended by Ace's casual question about whether or not she is married: the point here is that Ace does not judge either way[23]. (One

---

[22] Briggs, *The Curse of Fenric*, p62.

[23] *Ghost Light* too contains asides about 'Victorian values': the patriarchal 'family' unit of Gwendoline, Mrs Pritchard, and Josiah

might speculate how Kathleen's opinions affected her family life. Left widowed, she might be conscious of her child being fatherless, and keen to make clear that she was married. One wonders if her ideas were inherited by Audrey and become some of what Ace rebels against.) In the novelisation, we learn that Miss Hardaker was an unmarried mother: 'Only nineteen and with child – and she was unmarried. The looks, the whispers, the silences. A mother's pitying glances, and a father who never spoke another word to her until the day he died'[24]. Her shame has embittered her – one might even say has cursed her; this leads to her disastrous care of Phyllis and Jean, which drives them away from her and into the water[25].

It is interesting to compare all of this with the 2005 wartime story *The Empty Child / The Doctor Dances*: homosexual desire is shown on screen (Jack invites the Doctor to dance), and Nancy's unashamed statement of her love for her illegitimate son is what saves the world by enabling the nanobots to recognise parental DNA ('I am your mummy. I will always be your mummy'). A little later, however, *The Doctor, The Widow and the Wardrobe* (2011), by the same writer, gives us a highly sentimentalised depiction of motherhood in which Madge Arwell, through the fact of child-bearing, seems to have acquired a special, almost mystical quality. The story ends by reuniting Madge and her children with her husband and their father, restoring the nuclear family to its special and privileged position. This

---

Smith is a sham that corrupts both women; *Survival* deals if not frankly then certainly subtextually with lesbian desire.

[24] Briggs, *The Curse of Fenric*, p105.

[25] In the novelisation, Miss Hardaker accuses Phyllis and Jean of causing the deaths of two Home Guard, who have gone looking for them, thereby passing on her guilt and shame, passing on the 'curse' (Briggs, *The Curse of Fenric*, p92).

is a far cry from the harder, more realistic edge in *The Curse of Fenric*: Frank Dudman will not return from the war, but life will go on.

Andrew Cartmel did not succeed in his stated aim of bringing down the government; the slayers of the Tory Prime Minister would be the traditional enemy, her own colleagues. Post-2005, **Doctor Who** is able to be more explicitly socially liberal, but the programme's politics are in fact never as explicitly radical as those of the late 1980s. It's in this sense, then, that I can hardly believe that *The Curse of Fenric* exists. Prevailing institutional attitudes and the spirit of the times were against it. And yet – there it is, clever, complex, multivariate, and brought into existence in no time. Ambitious, honest, fast-paced, scary and radical, it is a joy to watch.

CHAPTER 2: DON'T MENTION THE WAR

Doctor Who in an Exciting Adventure With Nazis

It's a curious fact that *The Curse of Fenric* is the first **Doctor Who** story to have a Second World War setting. When one surveys the programmes one might have routinely watched during the period 1963-1989, and beyond, the absence becomes remarkable. Consider some of the following: **Colditz** (BBC, 1972-74); **Secret Army** (BBC, 1977-79); **Tenko** (BBC, 1981-84); **Enemy at the Door** (LWT for ITV, 1978-80); **Wish Me Luck** (ITV, 1988-90); *Blue Remembered Hills* (BBC, 1979); **Foyle's War** (ITV, 2002-15); **Fortunes of War** (BBC/WGBH (Boston)/Primetime Television for BBC, 1987); **'Allo, 'Allo** (BBC, 1982-1992); **It Ain't Half Hot, Mum** (BBC, 1974-81); **Goodnight, Sweetheart** (BBC, 1993-99); **Dad's Army** (BBC, 1968-77)... Across channels, from high-status elite one-off, to series, to comedy, to children's, the Second World War is a staple setting for postwar British television drama to this day[26].

What can we make of this absence in **Doctor Who**'s repertoire before 1989? The Second World War is, obviously, an influence on the programme's storytelling prior to this date: hardly surprising given the generation of creators involved, many of whom had served during the war. The 'base under siege' story is directly related to the submarine sub-genre (see *Cold War* (2013)); both the Cybermen and the Daleks permit thinly veiled allegories examining eugenics, totalitarianism, and genocide. There are of course Nazis in **Doctor Who** – they're just not literally present (they don't in fact appear in *The Curse of Fenric* either).

---

[26] Angelini, Sergio, 'WWII Dramas' provides a good primer.

What might have prevented the use of such a setting? That **Doctor Who** was a family programme, with younger viewers, was certainly no barrier to story-telling with a wartime setting, as productions such as **Carrie's War**[27], **The Diary of Anne Frank**[28], and **How We Used to Live**[29] demonstrate. It's obviously notable that the programmes I mention above are realist dramas[30], and some concern may have surrounded whether it was appropriate to use recent history as a backdrop for the Doctor's adventures. The shift in 1987 to a younger script editor (and the younger team of writers which Andrew Cartmel began to assemble around him) coincides with an attempt to use the Second World War more consciously as a source of storytelling. Nevertheless, there were plainly numerous sensitivities still at work. Cartmel recounts that for the previous season's *Silver Nemesis* (1988), producer John Nathan-Turner forbade any mention of Nazis:

> '[W]hen John read early drafts of the scripts, featuring a lot of action and involving Nazis, he freaked. The notion of neo-Nazis, latter-day fascists, seemed just too political and potentially controversial. He wouldn't have it. So I simply went through the script removing every mention of the word

---

[27] BBC, 1974; an adaptation of the 1973 novel by Nina Bawden, about two children evacuated to Wales to escape the Blitz.

[28] BBC, 1987. Katharine Schlesinger, who played Anne Frank, would appear in **Doctor Who** two years later as Gwendoline in *Ghost Light*.

[29] **How We Used to Live** was a children's educational historical drama, which, over the course of its run (BBC, 1968-2002), used family drama to portray British social and political history from the late Victorians to 1970. Series 4, broadcast 1981-1982, covered the period 1936-53.

[30] Angelini calls *Blue Remembered Hills* Potter's 'most straightforward and naturalistic play'.

"Nazi" [...] and substituting the word "Paramilitary" [...]. This did the trick, and John was happy.'[31]

Visually, however, it's no holds barred, not least as a result of the casting of Anton Diffring, Britain's favourite screen Nazi[32], as de Flores. Cartmel writes:

'[A]bsolutely no bones are made about de Flores' "Paramilitary" background, with a swastika paperweight on the desk, Wagner blaring from a gramophone on the balcony and a toast being proposed to the "Fourth Reich"'[33].

(I, for one, had not noticed that the word Nazi isn't used until it was pointed out to me. Don't mention the War indeed.)

As stories were being assembled for season 26, writer Ian Briggs pitched a story set during the Blitz that ultimately became *The Curse of Fenric*:

'Thinking back now, I'd moved from west London to east London soon after finishing *Dragonfire*, and was struck by the still remaining evidence of streets which had been obliterated in the Blitz – stories of carnage in Canning Town near where I was living.'[34]

But the rationale for producing a story with a wartime setting was

---

[31] Cartmel, Andrew, *Script Doctor*, p127-128.
[32] A sample from Diffring's resumé from the 1950s to the 80s of occasions when he played German officers or Nazis: *The Colditz Story* (1955), *The Heroes of Telemark* (1965), *Where Eagles Dare* (1968), *Operation Daybreak* (1975, as Reinhard Heydrich) and *The Winds of War* (1983, as Joachim von Ribbentrop).
[33] Cartmel, *Script Doctor*, p132.
[34] Personal communication with the author, April 2018.

less to do with filling a lacuna, and more to do with Cartmel's increasing understanding of what would work on screen given not only budgetary limitations, but which would also play to the strengths of the design staff:

> 'I'd already determined that Earth-based historical stories had the strongest chance of working onscreen. *Delta and the Bannermen, Remembrance of the Daleks* [1988], and the Elizabethan sections of *Silver Nemesis* had established that'[35].

Cartmel's production diary from the time recounts repeated examples of his frustration that the design of science fictional and futuristic settings not only consistently failed to come close to his vision, but critically undermined what he was trying to achieve: 'I was watching Ian's episode 1 [of *Dragonfire*] with him and aching – aching at the cheapness and nastiness with which it had been shot'[36]. Yet part of Cartmel's plan for the show was to return it to its science fictional roots. Describing the experience of watching episodes from Eric Saward's last season as script editor, he wrote:

> '[T]here was no feeling for science fiction or fantasy in the show at the point where I took over. Basically the scripts were failed thrillers full of confusing incident and boring characters with science fiction **detail** arbitrarily heaped on, but nothing genuinely science fictional about them.'[37]

As a result, in an attempt to make science fiction stories that were not ruined by poor design, Cartmel had brought about a general shift away from futuristic settings to stories requiring historical and

---

[35] Cartmel, *Script Doctor*, p164.
[36] Cartmel, *Script Doctor*, p85.
[37] Cartmel, *Script Doctor*, p81.

contemporary settings. The 26th season of **Doctor Who** keeps the need for science fictional design to a minimum: *The Curse of Fenric* and *Ghost Light* are both historicals; *Battlefield* and *Survival* both have contemporary settings. Gone are the over-lit studios and fright-wigs, staples for so many years. The base under siege is a Victorian haunted house.

Nevertheless Cartmel's frustrations at the apparent lack of ability to realise science fictional elements did not go away. Looking back at *Battlefield*, he writes:

> 'I was simply getting worn down by my constant struggle to make an intelligent science fiction drama in an environment which simply didn't understand science fiction. They **just didn't get it**. We were up against a culture of incomprehension. No matter how hard we tried or how good the scripts were, what ended up on the screen was all too often a travesty of our intentions.'[38]

In this case, it was a failure to understand that the knights should be wearing powered armour, on the lines of Heinlein's *Starship Troopers* (1959). The Haemovores, too, would prove a source of disappointment:

> 'Unfortunately, as so often happened, the rubber Haemovore masks that looked awe inspiring at rest became almost comical once attempts were made to animate them. In particular, the chief monster, the Ancient Haemovore, was risible. He stood in a tunnel, his gills pulsing and his eyes moving convincingly enough, but his jaw flapped helplessly

---

[38] Cartmel, *Script Doctor*, p150. Emphases in the original.

and comically during this, his big speech. Various bits of padding and sticky tape were applied to try and remedy it. I sighed and resigned myself to another near miss in the special effects.'[39]

Contemporary and historical settings provided the best chance of realising on screen the intentions of the writers and script editor.

There are, however, other constraints that a Second World War setting might place upon a narrative; constraints which hold true of any time-travel story with a historical setting, what as **Doctor Who** fans we might call – depending on our age – the Aztec problem, or the Vesuvius problem. This is the problem of telling a story set during known history. **Doctor Who** works out as early as its sixth story, *The Aztecs* (1964), that the fourth wall can bend only so far, and that known history cannot meaningfully be changed within the confines of the format. This dilemma is precisely what motors the plot of that story. The handful of later, purely 'historical'[40] stories use history chiefly as backdrop[41], or use the inevitability of the history to

---

[39] Cartmel, *Script Doctor*, p166.

[40] I find the usual distinction of 'historicals' (where the only fantastical element is the Doctor, the TARDIS, and the companions) and 'pseudo-historicals' (where another element, such as alien presence, is set alongside the historical setting), not particularly insightful when it comes to considering narrative choices made in stories with historical settings. History still has to remain the same, no matter how many Terileptils are hiding out around Pudding Lane. Speaking in terms of constructing plot and narrative, the aliens are present chiefly to provide the jeopardy, and to distract from questions surrounding the time travel.

[41] In many ways, Ancient Greece in *The Myth Makers* (1965), Ancient Rome in *The Romans* (1965), and the Wild West in *The Gunfighters*

foreground stories of individuals caught up in dramatic moments[42]. Look at *The Reign of Terror* (1964) and, most beautifully, *The Massacre* (1966), which derives great narrative power from Steven as a man multiply dislocated in time. A contemporary viewer, who, as James Cooray Smith has suggested[43], would be more likely to know this history, would not know whether or not Steven would survive. For 21st-century viewers, the likely comparative lack of knowledge of the setting adds to the uncertainty.

But where do we go from here? The imperative to leave known history intact is a problem for a storyteller, whose business is precisely the narration of change, and who must provide some jeopardy for the story to maintain interest of suspense[44]. I prefer to think in terms of narrative jeopardy than narrative conflict. In this I am completely influenced by Ursula Le Guin:

> Modernist manuals of writing often conflate story with conflict. This reductionism reflects a culture that inflates aggression and competition while cultivating ignorance of other behavioural options. No narrative of any complexity can be built on or reduced to a single element. Conflict is one kind of behaviour. There are others, equally important in any human life, such as relating, finding, losing, bearing,

---

(1966) might just as well be alien or fantastical settings.

[42] As a history undergraduate, I attended a lecture on the Massacre of St Bartholomew's Day given by an expert on the subject. Partway through recounting the events, he stopped, and said, 'Nobody's quite sure what happens now.'

[43] Cooray Smith, James, **Doctor Who**: *The Black Archive #2: The Massacre*

[44] Le Guin, Ursula K., *Steering the Craft*, p123.

discovering, parting, changing.

This storytelling dilemma is rehearsed again in *The Fires of Pompeii* (2008), where a rather clumsy explanation of 'fixed points in time' is used to extricate the Doctor and Donna from their moral dilemma, whilst simultaneously leaving the Doctor's moral authority intact as he causes the eruption of the volcano that will cause the death of thousands. Saving Caecilius and his family is presumably intended to act as emotional catharsis for the wider carnage. But with the plot so carefully contrived to limit the Doctor's field of action, one is almost left wondering why the story has been told at all[45].

To a great extent, the Doctor's function within any given narrative in **Doctor Who** is to be precisely that: the agent of change. The story that follows *The Fires of Pompeii*, *Planet of the Ood* (2008), is a much more successful examination of the limits of the Doctor's agency. The story, which was in production during commemorations of the 200th anniversary of the Slave Trade Act 1807, consciously evokes images reminiscent of the Middle Passage (the Ood caged for processing and transit); the displacement into a science fictional setting addresses issues of taste and sensitivity. It is striking, on viewing, how most of the significant acts that lead to the liberation of the Ood have taken place over years before the Doctor's arrival[46]: a subtle subversion of

---

[45] I have some nerve writing this, given my own short story, 'The Slave War', a Second Doctor story set during the Spartacus rebellion, which deals in exactly the same coin. McCormack, Una, 'The Slave War'. De Candido, Keith, ed, *Short Trips: The Quality of Leadership*, p41-62.

[46] The 'Friends of the Ood', who have had an undercover agent within Ood Operations for a decade, and the Ood themselves mount a rebellion against their owners. The Doctor fails to appeal to the better nature of Ood Operations employee Solana and also reflects

the standard **Doctor Who** story in which the Doctor arrives and brings about regime change (overnight, for example, in *The Happiness Patrol*). If *The Fires of Pompeii* overwrites the deaths and suffering of thousands with the Doctor's personal suffering, *Planet of the Ood* undercuts the Doctor's intervention entirely. To paraphrase Alan Bennett, history is not Great Men Acting Heroically but women and Ood, following with a bucket.

The trick, as any storyteller knows, is to make features out of bugs, and to turn the problem into the resolution. If known history (from the standpoint of the viewer, peering through the fourth wall) cannot be changed – even more imperative while the history is still within living memory or is subject to contemporary sensitivities – then other histories have to come into play, and different sources of narrative jeopardy need to be found. This is precisely what *The Curse of Fenric* does.

The historical moment chosen is one that presents history in flux. The Second World War is still underway but, given the dating of the story, 1943, the characters involved are already looking to the next war. The story notably avoids loading suspense onto the war setting. That history is fixed: the Axis powers will lose and the post-war consensus will emerge. What is primarily at stake is not the past and the present (whether viewing in 1989 or 2018), but the Earth's far future. This is the contest which the Doctor and Fenric are playing, not the immediate war being dramatised on screen. The choices made by the individual characters, whether they survive or not, are what will prevent the devastating pollution of the planet by Fenric's

---

on his own guilt in failing to grapple with the Ood's servitude during their last encounter in *The Impossible Planet / The Satan Pit* (2006).

servants. These choices are thematic: will the 'curse' which follows the Wolves of Fenric play out to its horrific and logical conclusion, or will the Wolves exercise individual will and choice to extricate themselves from the curse of their history?

The narrative therefore derives its suspense substantially from the story arcs of the individual characters, all of whom are bound up not only in the Curse, but in their own personal histories. Wainwright's sense of being insufficient to his task compared to his father and grandfather, for example, causes his crisis of faith. The novelisation, in particular, is illuminating in this respect, expanding the individual motivations of characters: Millington and Judson are bound together by the fact that Judson has been crippled by Millington's sexual jealousy; Miss Hardaker's shame and guilt leads to the deaths of Jean and Phyllis. The personal histories of these characters burden them; curse them. And then, of course, there is Ace's story. With the revelation that Kathleen Dudman, one of the Wrens stationed at the base, is Ace's grandmother, and that her baby is Ace's estranged mother, Ace's own personal history is woven into the apocalyptic battle. During the course of the story, Ace's movement towards forgiveness of her mother secures her own future, as the rest of the narrative dramatises the cumulative efforts of individuals to save Earth's future. The wartime setting of *The Curse of Fenric* is very far from being window-dressing, and the moment in the war chosen is crucial: a moment of inchoateness where familiar historical narratives are falling apart, and the cast and story of the new narrative are far from being set. Potential futures are being created in the apocalyptic crucible of total war.

In 1989, a similar rewriting of history was happening. Ian Briggs, reflecting on the genesis of the story, writes:

'[L]ooking back now, I realise that my travels in Sweden influenced the Fenric story in a way I never realised at the time. Sweden was a neutral country in the Cold War, so young people from Iron Curtain countries were allowed to visit there, and I met quite a few as I was travelling. And this quite obviously drew my imagination when I was developing *Fenric* to the possibilities in the Second World War being a point before the Iron Curtain fell, when the hostilities were more ambiguous – a period when the East and the West were notionally allies in war. My experience travelling in the neutral zone of Sweden led me to the strange shifting allegiances of the Second World War. Unwittingly I was channelling an impending zeitgeist, because a year later, halfway through the run of *Fenric*, the Berlin Wall fell. I don't think anyone noticed that the evening before, on the other side from **Coronation Street**, we'd been telling the same story. But I was stunned.'[47]

I noted in my discussion of *The Fires of Pompeii* how, in that story, the Doctor's individual suffering at times overwrites that of the thousands who suffered in the eruption. This is a risk with historical storytelling, particularly in **Doctor Who**, where the familiar characters in whom one is invested are, by virtue of the format, simply passing through. *The Curse of Fenric* does not make this mistake. Ace's emotional arc does not displace the history; indeed, her direct connection to what's happening during *The Curse of Fenric* imbues the story with more power, dramatising the still-living connection between the past and now. This is not always the case with **Doctor Who** stories that use a Second World War setting.

---

[47] Personal communication with the author, April 2018.

42

I became interested in seeing how other writers of **Doctor Who** negotiated the difficulties of placing a time-traveller into known – and still, barely, lived – history. My first surprise was how little the Second World War is used as a setting after 1989: three televised **Doctor Who** stories[48], *Captain Jack Harkness* (2007) from **Torchwood**, and *Lost in Time* (2010) from **The Sarah Jane Adventures**. Even expanding my scope into the ancillary material, such as spin-off novels and audio dramas, there was still surprisingly little: 9 novels, some with only a tangential use of the Second World War, and 13 audio dramas (plus a spinoff series). (I will discuss the ancillary texts briefly here: my purpose is to look at storytelling strategies within the format of **Doctor Who**, and the sample of Second World War stories is otherwise very limited.)

The narrative strategies used to generate story in the ancillary texts are fairly straightforward: these are generally pseudo-historicals in which tension is generated from whether or not the Doctor can prevent the incursion of some alien or other threat, such as Cybermen in *Illegal Alien*, or the Sidhe in *Autumn Mist*. The war setting is primarily used thematically. Some stories use closed settings to generate the 'base under siege': occupied Jersey, in the New Adventure *Just War*, or Colditz castle, in the audio set there. There's also a sub-genre in the novels of putting the Doctor alongside other 'Great Men': *The Turing Test* embroils him in a spy game

---

[48] These are: *The Empty Child / The Doctor Dances*, *Victory of the Daleks*, and *The Doctor, the Widow, and the Wardrobe*. I discuss the first two of these here, plus *Let's Kill Hitler*, which although it does not have a wartime setting, uses the visual language extensively. *The Doctor, the Widow, and the Wardrobe* is discussed in chapter 3.

involving Alan Turing, Graham Greene and Joseph Heller, in a subtle and literary novel. Andrew Cartmel's own *Atom Bomb Blues* takes the Doctor to Los Alamos where he meets Oppenheimer. In the second New Adventure *Timewyrm: Exodus* the Doctor is in Berlin confronting Hitler. Other tactics include making the known history work in the dramatist's favour: Ian Potter's audio play *The Alchemists* uses the Doctor's granddaughter Susan's haziness about human history to generate irony; my own audio play 'An Eye for Murder' uses Chamberlain's broadcast announcing the outbreak of war to shift the tone and trigger the action that drives the last part of the play. Most striking was the foregrounding of the personal narratives of the companions. Done successfully, the war setting worked dramatically and thematically, for example, in the short story 'Tell Me You Love Me', which takes the First Doctor's companion Barbara back to the Blitz to come to terms with the death of her father during the war[49]. In some cases, particularly during complex story arcs in the audio dramas, the war setting seems chiefly to be window-dressing for the companion's unfolding narrative – the war is used chiefly here as a means of emotional intensification (e.g. in the audio dramas *The Girl Who Never Was* for the Eighth Doctor's companion, Charlie Pollard; and *Dark Convoy* with Ace).

When **Doctor Who** returned to screen in 2005, the wartime setting seemed mainly to be used for emotional intensification. A successful example would be the **Torchwood** episode *Captain Jack Harkness*, in which the Blitz is used to intensify the emotional drama between both the Captains, but in doing so, writes a suppressed gay history. However, other examples are more problematic, for example, *Let's*

---

[49] Matthewman, Scott, 'Tell Me You Love Me' in Scott, Cavan, and Mark Wright, eds, *Short Trips: The Ghosts of Christmas*, pp35-47.

Kill Hitler (2011). (This episode, while set prewar, uses the visual trappings of Second World War stories, so I include it here.) It begins with a memorable regeneration by Amy and Rory's friend Mels into their daughter, and possibly wife of the Doctor, River Song. Firstly, however, she's waved a revolver at the Doctor and lampshaded the whole narrative problem to which most of this chapter is devoted: 'You've got a time machine – I've got a gun. Come on, let's kill Hitler!' With Hitler shoved unceremoniously in a cupboard near the start of the episode – and left there throughout – and Berlin's wealthy elite forced to run through the streets in their underwear, the episode is tapping into the same vein of farce that drives *The Producers*, *'Allo, 'Allo*, and, indeed, much wartime comedy. But what works there (more or less), is deeply uneasy here. The backdrop of 1930s Germany is primarily a means to establish River as the nastiest sociopath in town. The foregrounding of River's story plus a shift to farce is a displacement too far, and the secondary plot, in which a group of time-travelling vigilantes hunt down and execute war criminals, isn't sufficient to justify these moves. This is an uneasy episode, not entirely on the right side of good taste.

A similar problem troubles *Victory of the Daleks* (2010). Here the Doctor takes companion Amy to the Cabinet War Rooms, where he is horrified to discover the British have a new weapon – the Ironsides, no, Daleks. The episode plays with the familiar iconography of the war: the Dalek poster; a shot of British soldiers raising the Union Flag that calls to mind the famous photograph from Iwo Jima; Spitfires in space. Meanwhile, Churchill spouts familiar epigrams. Arguably, this is all part of a current trend to re-evaluate the nature of British preparedness: gone are the bumbling amateurs of **Dad's Army**, replaced by a government that seizes sweeping powers, plans use of chemical agents on the invasion beaches, and ruthlessly prepares to defeat the enemy at any cost. But, the tone is playful. Amy is visibly excited throughout; the death of the husband of a minor character is dealt with peremptorily (compare this the news of the death of Frank Dudman, which has real weight). This is history as tourism – visiting the war zone then moving on.

Ian MacNeice reprises his role as Churchill from *Victory of the Daleks* in the Big Finish series **The Churchill Years**. In the third episode of the first series, the TARDIS takes Churchill to Britain in 55 BCE, where Churchill meets Julius Caesar and, later, discovers the British are serving a cruel Bronze God, no, Dalek. Churchill, TARDIS, Caesar, Dalek: we are given a series of figures detached from context. While the plays are enjoyable, this is not Winston Churchill but a fictional character constructed from well-known sayings, vocal tics, and a desire for historical playfulness on the part of the authors. As in *The Wedding of River Song* (2011), Churchill becomes a figure floating free of history; a character from a story-book figuring large in the ongoing process of national myth-making about the war, bestriding both past and present like a colossus. Again, the overall effect is slightly uneasy.

I'll close this survey of the uses of the Second World War as source of storytelling in **Doctor Who** with two successes. *The Empty Child / The Doctor Dances* (2005) playfully places Rose in a Union Jack T-shirt and then sends her flying over London in the Blitz. But this is all grounded in (a kind of) reality. The story avoids nostalgia by hinting at abuse experienced by evacuee children, showing the gallows humour of drinking and laughing while bombs fall overhead, and by hinging the resolution of its plot on the acknowledgement by an unmarried mother of her illegitimate child. (As I discussed in Chapter 1, whatever future we're building, shaming single mothers is not part of it.) If the self-congratulatory tone is laid on a bit thick at the end, when the Doctor exhorts the people of London not to forget the Welfare State (and seems to charge Victor Meldrew personally with this responsibility), I am sufficiently partisan to find this kind of national myth-making uplifting fun rather than repellent nonsense. The tone is undercut by the truly frightening gasmask 'monsters', and a short effective scene between Nancy and Rose that brings home how the Blitz must have felt like the end of the world.

Perhaps inevitably, we have to look to the programme most like **Doctor Who** prior to 1989 to find a story that uses a wartime setting as successfully as *The Curse of Fenric*. In *Lost in Time* (2010), from **The Sarah Jane Adventures**, Sarah Jane's 'companion' Clyde finds himself in 1940s Britain, helping a small boy alert the local villagers to a party of Nazi spies who have landed on the south coast. (They are, helpfully and rather charmingly, in full uniform.) It's a simple story, firmly in the tradition of the children's wartime adventure, and Clyde is slightly hazy on the details ('We will fight them on the beaches! We will fight them on the other places!'), but when he returns to the present and looks up the boy, he discovers an old man, still alive, receiving an honour from the Queen for his work on radar. The plot itself is resolved when three old women work together, across time, to save the Earth, permitting the excellent line: 'You and your granny just saved the world!' All this builds up to an assertion of the value of older people entirely congruent with the main message of the show. It's an affirmation of the connectedness of the present to the past, and, with a light touch, emphasises the significance of our present actions in constructing the future.

What does it mean, to say that history is over? In the action of *The Curse of Fenric*, the first act of the Cold War is being initiated and the board is being set across Europe. As *The Curse of Fenric* was being written and transmitted, the last act of the Cold War was playing out and the European chess board was being re-laid. As I sit and write, in June 2018, the far right is on the rise again across Europe and the US, and the chess board at times seems to be on fire. That Fukuyama has been proven wrong is apparent, yet, rather than the end of history we now observe rather a tendency to collapse historical progress into a permanent now. **Doctor Who**'s use, in recent years, of historical settings as, in effect, tourist locations portrays history as a kind of a simultaneity, echoing the shift in postmodernism away from belief in the modernist project of progress. Will Davies writes:

> 'In place of a collective historical consciousness, in which the synchronous present is differentiated from both our past and our future, postmodernity offers only a spatial heterogeneity. There is no collective progress or radical emancipatory project understood in a historical sense, but simply a panoply of locations, scattered in space but never differentiated in time.'[50]

In 1989, in *The Curse of Fenric*, we saw instead a narration of utopia; the possibility of a future that is progressive; a maturation of both self and society. History, and, by implication, the future emerging from the past, is not closed down but opened up to the potential for change emerging from collective action.

We play the contest again.

---

[50] Davies, William, 'Introduction to Economic Science Fictions', p16. Davies, William, ed, *Economic Science Fictions*.

CHAPTER 3: FRIENDS OF DOROTHY

The Emotional Intensification of Doctor Who

The late, great feminist science fiction writer and critic, Joanna Russ, in her classic 1970 essay 'The Image of Women in Science Fiction'[51], charged science fiction with a lack of imagination and 'social speculation' when it came to writing women. What she saw instead was unbelievable female characters and clichés. This imaginative failure, Russ argued, was exactly the opposite of what science fiction should be about: 'science fiction writers have no business employing stereotypes, let alone swallowing them goggle-eyed'[52]. Russ memorably concluded: 'There are plenty of **images** of women in science fiction. There are hardly any women [my emphasis]'[53]. Russ's fuller body of work, fiction and non-fiction, extends this criticism to include girls and adolescent women, and, in this chapter, I will consider her arguments in relation to **Doctor Who**. There are of course a great number of adolescent girls and young women in **Doctor Who**: indeed, the presence of a 'girl' companion is almost part of the programme's format. I would suggest, however, following Russ, that very often these are images, and that there are in fact hardly any girls in **Doctor Who**. Ace, I will suggest, is one honourable exception, with *The Curse of Fenric* critical to her story.

Russ, in her essay, and in typically acerbic fashion, rapidly sketches and dispenses with the clichés of science fiction: the 'intergalactic suburbia' in which the 1950s household remains intact and the

---

[51] Russ, Joanna, 'The Image of Women in Science Fiction' in *The Country You Have Never Seen*, p205-218.
[52] Russ, 'Image of Women', p210.
[53] Russ, 'Image of Women', p217.

woman is wife, mother, and home-maker; the 'passive and involuntary' women as prizes or motives for space-faring 'He-Men'; and the domineering Amazons of matriarchies, waiting to be brought to heel by the arrival of men. Her most illuminating criticism for our purposes, however, is of Ursula K Le Guin's *The Left Hand of Darkness*. This novel, published in 1969, a Nebula Award winner and generally accepted to be ground-breaking in its treatment of gender, concerns the inhabitants of the planet Gethen, who have no sex or gender, except that every four weeks they pass through a cycle in which they become either male or female, and sexually potent. The story is motored by the arrival on Gethen of a male human observer, who becomes immersed in Gethenian culture and politics. Russ skilfully argues this is a book from which women are absent:

> 'It is, I must admit, a deficiency in the English language that these people must be called "he" throughout, but put that together with the native hero's personal encounters in the book, the absolute lack of interest in child-raising, the concentration on work, and what you have is a world of men.'[54]

(An aside on child-rearing: I am not saying that women are solely responsible for child-rearing. I **am** saying that child-rearing has been, and continues to be, primarily the responsibility of women and that, as a result, it is pushed into the private and domestic sphere rather than foregrounded in the public sphere. This goes for everyday life, and for fiction. In science fiction in particular, Russ is arguing, where action adventure predominates, the necessity of this work is not foregrounded. Where it **is** brought out of the private realm, where

---

[54] Russ, 'Image of Women', p215.

the burden of care is made visible and is given consideration – there, Russ says, we are more likely to find women and not their image in science fiction.)

Russ, in her own science fiction, writes not images, but women, most notably in her 1975 novel *The Female Man*, in which four women from parallel universes, brought together, disrupt each other's ideas of what it means to be a woman. In her earlier short story 'When It Changed' (1972)[55], Russ, having read Le Guin's novel, created the world of Whileaway, almost in response to Le Guin's Gethen[56], where there are no men. They have died out 30 generations ago, leaving a colony of women who are people – active, neither masculine nor feminine, since such distinctions are meaningless. Just as significantly, for my purposes, Russ creates memorable adolescent girls – children on the cusp of womanhood, learning what it means to be women. In her novel *The Two of Them* (1978), galactic time agent Irene rescues a girl, Zubeydeh, from a male-dominated world where women live in purdah. In rescuing Zubeydeh, Irene exiles herself from the time agency and goes into hiding in 1970s America, where she will have to live with the sexism of the time, hoping for an improvement for Zubeydeh, but haunted by the possibility that the girl will be crushed, as was her aunt, Dunyazad: 'that mad, dead, haunted woman who could not tell stories, who could not save herself.'[57] Conversely, in 'When it Changed', the narrator describes her daughter, Yuriko, as dreaming 'twelve-year-old dreams of love and war: running away to sea, hunting in the north, dreams of

---

[55] This appeared in Harlan Ellison's edited collection *Again, Dangerous Visions* (1972).
[56] Russ, 'Afterword' to 'When It Changed'.
[57] Russ, *The Two of Them*, p181.

strangely beautiful people in strangely beautiful places...'[58]. I think of Ace when I read this, walking away from us at the end of *Survival* to see 'worlds [...] where the sky is burning, and the sea's asleep, and the rivers dream; people made of smoke and cities made of song,' and I think of Rose, running with delight towards the newly open doors of the TARDIS, in search of a different and a better way to live her life. When I think of Irene and Zubeydeh, making their escape across time, I think of the first Doctor and Susan – but Irene's escape routes are narrowed down immediately, a pessimistic if more realistic view of what can happen to a girl's dreams.

Where do these dreams lead? Do they in fact bring 'excitement, adventure, and really wild things'? Or do they go nowhere? What possibilities are available to a young female protagonist? What do girls get to do? Russ, in her essay 'What Can a Heroine Do?'[59], poses exactly this question, asking what myths, plots, and actions are available to a woman protagonist? Her answer is 'very few':

> 'The tone may range from grave to gay, from the tragedy of *Anna Karenina* to the comedy of *Emma*, but the myth is always the same: innumerable versions of Falling In Love, on courtship, on marriage, on the failure of courtship and marriage. How She Got Married. How She Did Not Get Married (always tragic). How She Fell In Love and Committed

---

[58] Since 'When it Changed' ends with the arrival of men on Whileaway, and the sense that a cold wind of change is coming as a result, we are left fearful for Yuriko's future, and whether her sense of limitless freedom will survive the coming years intact.

[59] Russ, J, (1995) 'What Can a Heroine Do? or Why Women Can't Write' in *To Write Like a Woman: Essays in Feminism and Science Fiction*. Bloomington: Indiana University Press.

Adultery. How She Saved Her Marriage But Just Barely. How She Loved a Vile Seducer And Eloped. How She Loved a Vile Seducer, Eloped, And Died in Childbirth.'[60]

The 'problem' of women in science fiction, according to Russ, is therefore twofold: the lack of women and girls (as opposed to images) in science fiction (a problem of representation), and also the poverty of stories available to them (a problem of agency).

I have spent some time discussing Joanna Russ because I believe her work provides carefully thought through ideas which are relevant when it comes to reflecting upon the role of the companion in **Doctor Who**. Russ outlines a double test for science fiction: a test of **presence** (are women and girls present, or are they instead substantially images?) and of **possibility** (do these women and girls get to act, or do they function passively, as prize, motive, or prop for a male protagonist?). Science fiction, Russ is arguing, as a literature concerned with speculation, should be a source of storytelling about girls and women which pushes the boundaries of what they are able to be and to do, rather than limiting them to a part where they facilitate the adventures of others until the inevitable conclusion of marriage and motherhood, closing the door on adventures of their own.

With all this in mind, let's turn to **Doctor Who**, to the companion in general, and to Ace in particular. On first sight, Ace appears to be very much in the mould of the typical companion. James Cooray Smith writes that:

'The archetypal **Doctor Who** companion is a fashionable

---

[60] Russ, 'What Can a Heroine Do?', p84.

woman from contemporary Earth (often contemporary London) who is attractive to the audience both as an identification figure and, frankly, an object of lust. She usually has a (sometimes frustrated) desire to do great things, a complicated family background and is strongly empathetic in order to provide a contrast with the more alien aspects of the Doctor [...] Most casual viewers of modern **Doctor Who** would recognise this as a description of Rose, Martha, Donna, Amy and Clara, but it also applies to Ace, Peri, Tegan, Polly, Jo Grant and Sarah Jane Smith.'[61]

Doctor Who most certainly passes the test of presence, and in companions such as Barbara, Liz, Sarah Jane, Romana, and Tegan, we clearly see women and not images. I would argue, however, that Ace represents a significant advancement in terms of **possibility**, i.e. in terms of her narrative, that this goes unmatched until the companions of the post-2005 era, and, in significant ways, surpasses them.

Ace is unusual in the pre-1989 era in having a sustained narrative, and even more unusual in that this is not preoccupied with romance and marriage. Ace's story is of the maturation of an adolescent girl, of the move from girlhood to womanhood. Her story is profoundly concerned with the role models available to young women, and the kinds of mentorship that they received, i.e. with aspects of child-rearing. This is in a genre that traditionally is more concerned with the dynamics of father-son relationships or of a boy's apprenticeship

---

[61] Cooray Smith, *The Massacre*, p138-9. He also shows how Dodo is the first character to demonstrate any aspects of this character type, 'making her one of the most important characters in the entire history of **Doctor Who**' (p140).

to a male master[62]. *The Curse of Fenric* is a pivotal moment in a season prominently concerned with Ace's maturation.

It's notable that the companions I mentioned above **don't** end their adventures handed over in marriage by the Doctor to a passing eligible male, as if their time in the TARDIS were one long waltz up the aisle. Barbara returns to her time with Ian; Liz goes back to Cambridge; Sarah Jane resumes a successful career[63]; Romana remains in E-Space; Tegan (whose time in the TARDIS is surely amongst the bleakest) returns to Earth disenchanted and traumatised. But the number of companions who end up paired off is striking: Susan, Vicki, Jo, Leela, Peri, and most bizarrely Mel with Glitz in *Dragonfire* ('Perhaps,' ponder the authors of *The Discontinuity Guide*, 'she fancies a bit of rough'[64]). Examples post-2005 include Rose and, most outrageously, Donna (eventually). It does not happen to the male companions, whose exits include death (Adric); return to their own time, either willingly or unwillingly (Ian, Ben, Jamie, Harry, Adam); or taking up the responsibility of rule (Steven, Turlough)[65]. Ace, in episode 3 of *The Curse of Fenric*,

---

[62] There is a reason that female fans have wept for joy to see *Star Wars'* Rey and *Black Panther's* Shuri!

[63] Recasting Sarah Jane's time in the TARDIS as a period of unrequited love that leaves her unable to form a long-term relationship, coupled with the sexual jealousy and competition between her and Rose, is an almost unforgiveable aspect of *School Reunion* (2006). This is redeemed significantly by her 'found family' and self-directed adventures in **The Sarah Jane Adventures**.

[64] Cornell, Paul, Martin Day and Keith Topping, *The Doctor Who Discontinuity Guide*, p 339

[65] See below for a brief discussion of Rory in the context of the Pond-Williams family.

acknowledges that marriage might be in her future: 'I used to think I'd never get married. Now I'm not so sure.' The point is that it is one choice amongst many, and that she is not being held back by anger or unhappiness. (It is particularly poignant that it is said to Kathleen, her grandmother, since her previous rejection of marriage was presumably in part to avoid recreating the dynamics of her relationship with her mother.)

It's important here not to overstate the crafting of Ace's story in the way that the stories of post-2005 companions have been crafted. Ian Briggs, recalling the writing of *The Curse of Fenric*, states that there was not a conscious attempt to write an arc for Ace:

> 'Ace herself was older, a nascent young woman growing out of the truculent, spirited teenager. I don't think I ever thought about that explicitly. Either a character goes on a journey, or they remain trapped in some kind of etherised stasis and turn into a caricature of themselves. Ace's journey was never planned, nor was the Doctor's – these revealed themselves as the story unfolded and the characters responded. For me, it's the story that catalyses the character journeys – although I know other writers work differently and start with character'.[66]

The shifting around in transmission order to place *The Curse of Fenric* after *Ghost Light*, in order to put the transmission of *The Curse of Fenric* closer to Hallowe'en, also indicates how loosely the arc was conceptualised. It's worth noting nevertheless that Aldred talks

---

[66] Personal communication with the author, April 2018.

about playing the character slightly differently – 'a little more disillusioned' – by *Survival*: the character's arc is there in the performance[67].

Ace's story, therefore, emerged organically, from themes already evident during this period, from the arrival of a new script editor and new writers, and from the positive dynamic of the whole creative team. By season 26, Ace has come to the forefront of the narrative: she is 'effectively the pivotal character in three of the season's four stories, and Sophie Aldred was given an early opportunity to talk to the writers about the development of the part'[68]. Nevertheless, Ace's stories, viewed in retrospect, provide the first notable example of a meaningful forward trajectory for a companion, a feature which will become standard post-2005. Her stories are also arguably the moment where the companion begins to shift towards being both a focalising character and one whose personal story is integral to the concept of the show[69].

Ace emerged initially from discussions between Nathan-Turner and Cartmel around the start of 1987, after Bonnie Langford announced her intention to leave during the course of that season. Cartmel wanted a strong, independent young woman in contrast to Mel: 'We

---

[67] 'Little Girl Lost' (extra on the *Survival* DVD).
[68] Howe, David J, Stephen James Walker and Mark Stammers, *The Handbook: The Unofficial and Unauthorised Guide to the Production of Doctor Who, Volume Two*, p481
[69] When it was announced that Billie Piper was to leave, there were many online debates from viewers who had come to **Doctor Who** in 2005 about whether the show could in fact survive her departure. To some, particularly new female viewers, Rose was seen as part of the format of the show: one could more easily and evidently replace the Doctor.

wanted a post-*Alien* teenage girl'[70]. Ace evolved from a character called Alf, whom Nathan-Turner and Cartmel had sketched in a description dated 16 January 1987[71].

Chief amongst Ace's antecedents is graphic novel heroine Halo Jones, created by Alan Moore, who first appeared in *2000 AD*[72]. (Teenager Halo Jones runs away from her boring space suburb to work as a stewardess on a space liner, and has various adventures, including becoming a space marine, historical legend, and deserter. There are later parallels in Ace's trajectory in the **New Adventures** novels.) Howe, Walker, and Stammers write: 'Cartmel was a big fan of contemporary comics, and was keen to bring that influence to **Doctor Who**. Collections of Alan Moore's **Halo Jones** stories from *2000 AD* consequently became virtually required reading for prospective **Doctor Who** writers'[73]. Cartmel, in his production diary for *Dragonfire*, describes the genesis of Ace thus: 'this wonderful anarchic teenager Ian [Briggs] had written, who sort of grew out of a Cockney checkout girl from a storyline I'd invented in January [1987] that was scrapped and changed'[74]. Briggs notes some of the changes that he made to 'Alf': moving her from North London to avoid having a trendy teenager from Islington, changing the name, and creating a personality (based on three teenage girls that he knew)[75], with

---

[70] Howe, Walker, Stammers, *The Handbook Volume Two*, p478
[71] Howe, Walker, Stammers, *The Handbook Volume Two*, p478
[72] *2000 AD* Prog 376, 7 July 1984
[73] Howe, Walker, and Stammers, *The Handbook Volume Two*, p 476
[74] Cartmel, *Script Doctor*, p77.
[75] Two of whom attend the recording of *Dragonfire*, Wednesday 12 August 1987:

> 'Ian had invited two guests to the studio, two teenage girls from the drama class he taught who were reportedly his

particular emphasis on loneliness[76]: '[A] trait that struck me as fairly typical of teenagers. They feel as though they don't quite recognise themselves and everything isn't as it ought to be'[77].

Cartmel's own first sight of 'Ace' is:

> 'Tuesday 14 April 1987. Ian [Briggs] delivered his second episode [of *Dragonfire*] in the usual London Business School brown envelope. This one had "Episode Two – read it and weep. PS. Has this been commissioned yet?" written on it. Ian's script was brilliant, with his "Crewmen/Women" (equal opportunity among futuristic space thugs; it was so nice and right and I wouldn't have thought of it). And then there was his fabulous character Ace, making exclamations like "doughnut!" and "Mega!" Ace was great. I suspected that she might end up being the new companion when Bonnie left.'[78]

So it proved (although the production team had also seriously considered Ray, played by Sara Griffiths, from *Delta and the Bannermen*). The choice to make Ace the companion seems partly to have arisen as a result of the casting of Sophie Aldred. Cartmel writes: 'Although Sara Griffiths was in the running for a while, it looked as though Sophie was going to be the companion'[79]. Once Aldred was cast, she in turn began to influence the character. Ace's

---

models of Ace. "Would you like to meet Bonnie Langford?" we asked them. "No, we'd like to meet Phillip Schofield"' (Cartmel, *Script Doctor*, p83.)

[76] Howe, Walker, and Stammers, *The Handbook Volume Two*, p478
[77] Quoted in Howe, Walker, and Stammers, *The Handbook Volume Two*, p486
[78] Cartmel, *Script Doctor*, p75.
[79] Cartmel, *Script Doctor*, p82.

look was in part adapted after she was cast:

> 'An actress called Sophie Aldred was there to play Ace [...]
> Sophie turned up in shorts and Doc Martens and she looked
> good in them. I asked Richard Croft, the costume designer, if
> she could wear the DMs when she was Ace as well'[80].

Briggs has stated: 'Andrew and John created the original character
(so the BBC owns the copyright), I created the personality, and
Sophie brought the character to life'[81].

Ace's character was formalised in August 1987 in a two-page
character guide intended to be supplied to prospective writers[82]. This
guide establishes her name, her age (16 years and 11 months)
(although she acts rather more like a 14-year-old), gives her home as
Perivale, and her difficult relationship with her parents. Her slang
(and tendency to call the Doctor the 'Professor') are noted, and her
personality outlined: 'Typical teenager really. Bright and full of life
one moment, spiky and argumentative the next.'[83] Ace bounces from
the page. This character guide arrived with Cartmel on 19 October
1987:

> 'On Monday, there was a letter from Ian Briggs waiting at the
> office. It included a sheet of character notes on Ace for the
> next season's writers. "I feel as if I'm giving away my only

---

[80] Cartmel, *Script Doctor*, p77.
[81] Quoted in Howe, Walker, and Stammers, *The Handbook Volume Two,* p486
[82] Howe, Walker, and Stammers, *The Handbook Volume Two,* p478
[83] Ian Briggs, quoted in Howe, Walker, Stammers, *The Handbook Volume Two,* p479

child," said Ian. "Look after her please."[84].

What makes Ace so different and satisfying a character? Her story, as I've already stated, is of the maturation of an adolescent girl. It traces the shift from disaffected teenager to mature young woman, taking on themes such as sexual awakening and experimentation, the possibilities available to young women, the kinds of mentorship that they receive, and the necessary psychological journey of separation from parents and authority figures. These themes begin to emerge early on during Ace's stories, and have pivotal moments during season 26 in general and *The Curse of Fenric* in particular.

Let's explore all this in more depth. In Ace's first full story as companion, *Remembrance of the Daleks*, she falls for Sergeant Smith, only to be betrayed. Her sexual awakening continues throughout season 26. In *Ghost Light*, Gwendoline models a form of adolescent female sexuality warped into seductiveness; in *Survival*, Ace experiments with lesbianism, and in *The Curse of Fenric*, her sexuality is extensively explored, through metaphors of deep water and swimming: Phyllis and Jean, as Haemovores, reminiscent of Le Fanu's *Carmilla* (1871-72), invite her 'into the water' (Ace refuses); she falls in love with Sorin, and this is reciprocated (but prevented by the Curse, and the hint of incest implied by that); and, finally, she consciously uses her sexuality as a tool for her own ends, initiating a sexual encounter with Sergeant Leigh for the Doctor's purposes. I seem to be rare in finding this scene wonderful; complaints seem to surround Sophie Aldred's age and the mannered dialogue[85]. While

---

[84] Cartmel, *Script Doctor*, p85.
[85] See Wood, Tat *About Time 6: The Unauthorized Guide to Doctor Who, 1985-1989*, p334

I'm baffled that anyone might be watching **Doctor Who** for naturalism, the scene works for me on its own terms. Ace makes all the running, making this a pivotal moment in which she demonstrates her agency. In a story concerned with possession and domination, Ace asserts her right to make her own choices about her body. *The Curse of Fenric* ends with Ace brought to a full awareness of what her adult sexuality might imply, without any sense that this will bring inevitable constraint, but with a full sense of potential dangers ahead. Ace is now ready to navigate deeper water. '[T]he depths of Lulworth Cove [...] stand not just for sexuality but for maturity'[86]. Ace speaks truly when she tells the Doctor that she is not a little girl any more.

Crucially, however, Ace's story is not leading inevitably towards marriage, although, as she states in *Fenric*, it's no longer off the table. Ace's narrative is about showing her new possibilities. Marriage and children become one possible choice among many. Here, as I've suggested already, she is unusual among companions. Even in the post-2005 era, the companion can still end her adventures at the altar (or equivalent): Rose is handed over to a substitute Doctor; Donna's story is bookended with weddings; River Song, too, is oddly domesticated. Compare and contrast with Amy, the girl who gets to have it all. Martha Jones, too, has a more interesting and complex arc: although she is plainly infatuated with the Doctor, this is explored more as a disciple's obsession with a charismatic and almost cultish figure from whose not entirely healthy influence Martha has to break free.

Central to Ace's story too is her relationship to the authority figures

---

[86] Cartmel, *Script Doctor*, p168.

in her life (the ur-story for teenagers, newly capable but deeply inexperienced) and particularly her mother. The character notes that Briggs supplied go into some detail:

> 'She didn't get on with her parents, and she gets angry simply at the mention of them. Sometimes she refuses to accept that she even has any parents; at other times she wants to believe that her "real" parents – the kind, loving ones – are somewhere else, maybe on another planet. But however bad a picture she paints of them, the truth is that her parents are an ordinary middle-class couple who always kept their feelings hidden, and didn't know how to cope with their tearaway daughter.'[87]

Throughout Ace's stories, we are shown repeated examples of relationships between mentor/parent/authority figures and young adults which are, in effect, offered to Ace as potential models for her own relationships to adults in her life. Most of these are unhealthy: Belazs and Kane in *Dragonfire*, Mags and the Captain in *The Greatest Show in the Galaxy* (1988), Gwendoline and Mrs Pritchard in *Ghost Light*, Paterson and his doctrine of 'survival of the fittest', taught to the children in his self-defence classes in *Survival*.

This theme is central to *The Curse of Fenric*. Indeed, the whole notion of a 'curse' is partly a means to explore the influence of one's history and ancestors upon one's present situation and psychology. The attempt to break a curse thereby becomes the attempt to liberate oneself from both structural circumstance and the impact of upbringing upon one's freedom to act. Almost all of the characters

---

[87] Ian Briggs, quoted in Howe, Walker, Stammers, *The Handbook Volume Two*, p479

wrestle with this 'curse': that is, the influence of authority figures and those who would direct or have already directed their lives. Phyllis and Jean are, in part, pushing against and therefore the victims of the mean-spirited guardianship of Miss Hardaker, which is punitive rather than protective. Wainwright, living in the long shadow of his father and grandfather, cannot summon sufficient internal resources to combat the curse. Nurse Crane's abuse of her physical power and authority over Judson results in her death at the hands of Fenric. (The toxic relationship between Millington and Judson can be read as a critique of the substitute parenting supplied by their public school.) The Ancient One, Ingiger, the product and slave of Fenric, has to break free of Fenric's authority in order to prevent the creation of the future in which the Earth is destroyed. And, of course, the consequences of this 'curse' upon Ace are central to *The Curse of Fenric* and beautifully dramatised. Ace is yet another of the Wolves of Fenric, and falls within the reach of the curse:

SORIN/FENRIC

The baby. In thirty years, the baby will be grown. She will have a daughter. That daughter will be you. You've just created your own future.

SORIN/FENRIC HOLDS AUDREY'S PHOTOGRAPH IN FRONT OF ACE.

The baby is your mother. The mother you hate.

In order to overcome the workings of the curse – that is, how the past seeks to direct our present choices and thus our future possibilities – Ace must come to terms with the reality of her mother, and not the image that she has been carrying with her, and which drives her to acts of destructiveness, and anger (her rejection of the

64

baby Audrey based on the name, rather than the reality of the child in front of her). In seeing her mother as a person in her own right, allowing the real baby Audrey to recast the imaginary mother who has had such power over Ace's choices in life, Ace is able to make the decisions and take the actions which save Kathleen and Audrey, thereby securing her own existence and future. In coming to terms with her mother as the person that she is, rather than the power that she has held, Ace takes a crucial step towards maturation. The fantasy she describes to Mel in *Dragonfire*, of being carried off to her 'real mum and dad' is replaced by reality: 'Mum, I'm sorry!'

Ace must also break her unshaken faith in her 'Professor'. Rather like a PhD supervisor, Ace's 'Professor' nurtures, teaches, acts as therapist, and forces the break when the student is independent. The 'education of Ace' by the Doctor was consciously written, partly at the suggestion of Sylvester McCoy:

> 'When we chatted between seasons, I thought it would be good for Ace to be educated between adventures. I would be educating her, pointing things out. Each time we got to a story, she would arrive with new knowledge [...] It was a good idea, and the writers went further, and John Nathan-Turner too. They decided the Doctor was trying to make her get over her fears, her weaknesses. The Doctor, in a very back-handed and subtle way, is trying to put Ace straight, so that eventually, if he does leave her she'll come back and be Prime Minister...!'[88]

In 1953, the British paediatrician and psychoanalyst Donald Winnicot coined the phrase 'the good-enough mother'. Winnicot argues that

---

[88] Sylvester McCoy, quoted in Howe, Walker, Stammers, *The Handbook Volume Two*, p480

perfect parenting, as well as being an impossibility, is in fact detrimental to a child's maturation. The limitless care that the newborn requires gives the necessary first experience of unconditional love; however, it's where parents fail, in tolerable ways, that provide the child with the ability to function maturely in the world, to cope with frustration, boredom, etc., and to see these not as potentially ego-destroying, but as part of the warp and weft of life. Ace has already seen her mother in a new light, the vulnerability of the baby allowing her to see her mother as the person she is; she must also learn to see the Doctor differently. Hence the critical moment in *The Curse of Fenric* where the Doctor intentionally breaks her faith in him in order to break the psychic barrier preventing the Ancient One from destroying Fenric (a moment which immediately follows on from the emotional shock Ace has received from learning the identity of the baby). Ace's blind faith here is a mistake: the Doctor cannot provide limitless care and love. This is a hard scene to watch, wonderfully played by McCoy and Aldred. Its point is to give Ace power and agency within her relationship with the Doctor. She is no longer wholly dependent; she can now see him in the same light as other adults in her life, realistically, as flawed individuals who may nevertheless be sources of advice or guidance, but who cannot be limitless sources of love, because such people do not exist, they are images. Coming to terms with this, learning to love people for who they are rather than for what they can provide us, is to mature.

I hope I have shown how, on a fundamental level, this period of **Doctor Who**, and *The Curse of Fenric* in particular, brings themes of mentorship and child-rearing to the fore. The story satisfies completely in this respect by showing the struggles that Kathleen Dudman faces in trying to do her job whilst caring for a very small child with very limited support. Compare this to the sentimentalism of wartime motherhood in *The Doctor, the Widow, and the Wardrobe*. Kathleen's husband will not return in time for Christmas. Kathleen's stoicism and resourcefulness are contrasted to Miss Hardaker's failure to protect Phyllis and Jean. Ace's faux pas in asking whether Kathleen is married and subsequent embarrassment are not an assertion of the primacy of the nuclear family[89], but ground Kathleen's character further in her time and place. Ian Briggs states:

> '[It wasn't] intentional to write significant women characters – I simply went for characters who could reveal interesting layers to the story. In the late-70s David Hare and Ian McEwan had written stage and TV dramas set in WW2 with a focus on the role of women in the war effort[90]; and I'd heard family stories of women's role back home, as well as personal stories of evacuees and their sometimes displaced, intrusive relationship with the local community – so it was entirely natural to find all kinds of characters and relationships drawn

---

[89] If we're in any doubt about whether this period of **Doctor Who** comes down on the side of the nuclear family, we need only look at the hideous and corrupting relationships between Josiah, Mrs Pritchard, and Gwendoline in *Ghost Light*.

[90] Hare, David (1985) *Plenty* (which concerns the postwar disillusionment of Susan Traherne, a former secret agent, now struggling with her unhappy domestic life and marriage); McEwan, Ian (BBC, 1980) *The Imitation Game* (which concerns a 19-year-old girl, Cathy Raine, who takes a job at Bletchley, and is destroyed by the experience). The BBC TV play of *The Imitation Game* foregrounds the female character, with a character, Turner, based loosely on Turing; the later film of the same name, *The Imitation Game* (2014), of course foregrounds Turing.

in by the Fenric story.'[91]

We are used to the story of Bletchley Park being associated with Alan Turing, and his subsequent status in gay historiography. However, Bletchley also inspired another sub-genre of wartime drama concerned with the invisibility of women's wartime work, their professionalisation during wartime and their subsequent removal from such professions, e.g. Ian McEwan's *The Imitation Game*, mentioned above, and **The Bletchley Circle** (ITV, 2012-; set post-war, but concerned with the wartime experience). Women constituted roughly 75% of the workforce at Bletchley (and were a significant number of the photographic interpreters at RAF Medmenham, where aerial photographic intelligence was analysed). In choosing a wartime setting reminiscent of Bletchley, which has obvious dramatic potential, Briggs also, whether intentionally or not, ensures the presence of women in his script.

At the end of her televised adventures, in *Survival*, Ace and her Professor are journeying onwards with places to see – and, most importantly, work to do. Ace's afterlife in the ancillary material novels and audios offers a number of alternative futures for her. In the epilogue of the novelisation of *The Curse of Fenric*, set in Paris in 1887, 'a young lady and an older gentleman' (Ace and the Doctor) stroll together through the Jardin des Tuileries[92]. Here Ace reveals that she is romantically involved: 'He's a young count from St Petersburg – Count Sorin. He's the perfect image of his great-grandson. And I think I've fallen hopelessly in love with him.'[93] Briggs

---

[91] Ian Briggs, personal communication with the author, April 2018.
[92] Briggs, *The Curse of Fenric*, p186.
[93] Briggs, *The Curse of Fenric*, p188.

also indicates motherhood in Ace's future:

> 'I would like to have done another story. I did have another
> idea for finishing Ace off. The final scene had Ace, now known
> as Dee, or something like that, aged about 30, putting her new
> baby to bed. In the mirror she sees in the doorway of the
> bedroom and there is the Doctor, just standing there watching
> her. She turns around and he's gone and she doesn't know if
> he was really there or if she was just imagining it. From the
> idea that she creates her own future and the baby in *Fenric*
> was her mother, I wanted to take that one generation further
> and get and get another reflection that in some obscure,
> convoluted way tied it up in an even neater package than it
> did.'[94]

These quiet, domestic moments contrast (though do not necessarily
contradict) the plans in season 27 for Ace to become a Time Lord. In
the projected story 'Ice Time', to be written by Marc Platt, Ace and
the Doctor would meet the Ice Warriors. The events of the story
would eventually be revealed to be a test by the Time Lords to see if
Ace was capable of entering the Prydonian Academy, a test which
Ace passes[95]. Sophie Aldred was greatly in favour of this conclusion
for Ace: '[I]t would have explained why the Doctor was doing all this
stuff with her'[96]. The story was eventually dramatised by Big Finish

---

[94] Ian Briggs, quoted in Aldred, Sophie, and Mike Tucker, *Ace! The
Inside Story of the End of An Era*, p64.
[95] Tarry, James, 'Doctor Who Episodes and Spin-Offs that Never
Happened.' *Den of Geek*, June 2011. How this squares with the desire
to remove the accumulated internal mythology I am not quite clear.
[96] 'Little Girl Lost'.

as *Thin Ice* in 2011[97], in which Ace refuses the opportunity to enter the Academy and continues travelling with the Doctor. In the **New Adventures**, Ace stops in the 26th century to join Spacefleet and fight Daleks; she travels again with the Doctor and Bernice Summerfield in both novels and then in audio plays, in which she eventually joins the Academy, travels with the Doctor and Mel, and joins the Celestial Intervention Agency before being returned to Earth with her knowledge of Gallifrey and the Time War removed[98]. In the *Doctor Who Magazine* strip, she is killed in an explosion[99]. In retrospect, leaving Ace as we do in *Survival* with her future open-ended is more satisfying than any conclusion: on the cusp of womanhood, anything is possible for this companion.

Russell T Davies has described the history of television as one of the increasing emotionalisation of stories: '[Y]ou look at the 60s and everything was **Man in a Suitcase** and **Randall and Hopkirk** – there was not an emotion to be spared. They were larks, adventures. By the 1980s, telly was wising up'[100]. And this emotional intensification is certainly present in the Davies era of **Doctor Who**: big emotional beats closely interwoven with the musical score. Now on **Doctor Who** we see the homes and families of companions, more than ever before: Jackie, Mickey, Wilf, etc., the Doctor folded into these families as much as he interrupts them. This is often used as a criticism of Davies' writing: the intrusion of the domestic sphere into **Doctor Who** is not only an emotional intensification but a

---

[97] Unrelated to the 2017 TV story of the same name by Sarah Dollard.
[98] *Love and War, Lucifer Rising, A Life of Crime*, **Gallifrey**: *Intervention Earth*, and **Gallifrey**: *Soldier Obscura* respectively.
[99] 'Ground Zero' *Doctor Who Magazine* 238-242.
[100] Marson, *JN-T*, p162.

'soapification' which turns a series whose 'proper' subject matter is adventure, science, and exploration into a programme more concerned with exploring emotions and relationships[101]. There are many instances in the post-2005 period where emotional beats and orchestral swells stand in place for the thorough working-through of plot. Nevertheless, I would argue that despite this, and despite the problems with some of the narrative arcs of female companions in the post-2005 era, this emotional intensification allows **Doctor Who** to more reliably show women and girls rather than their images, to permit their full participation in these adventure stories. This culminates most triumphantly in the story of Amy Pond, for whom the wedding day is not the conclusion of her story, but the moment when she asserts her right to both childhood dreams and an active adult life, who pulls the Doctor into her adventure and life (and family) at least as much as he pulls her away from hers[102].

---

[101] Condemnation of soap opera stands in a long tradition of demeaning women's speech and affairs as 'gossipy' and trivial, in contrast to the serious business of the (masculine) public sphere. There is a long-standing and robust field of feminist scholarship into soap opera, investigating themes of representation, active audiences, etc. An important first example of this field is Ang, Ien (1985) *Watching Dallas: Soap Opera and the Melodramatic Imagination*; a good survey of the field is Brunsdon, Charlotte (2000) *The Feminist, the Housewife and the Soap Opera*. Joanna Russ has no difficulty explaining how women's speech and writing are demeaned: see her legendary long essay *How To Suppress Women's Writing*.

[102] Through the enmeshing of Pond-Williams family with the Doctor's timeline which culminates in the Doctor becoming Amy and Rory's son-in-law, it's arguable that Amy is not so much a companion to the Doctor's adventures as he becomes a companion to hers. Rory, in this

Ace is the bridge for this: the moment where the companion begins to have a story of her own, the moment when the right of the women and girls to participate in the adventure on their own terms and not as prize or prop or motive is first asserted. Ace is not only present, she represents possibility.

---

reading, becomes an interesting spin on the male companion, married to Amy (rather than the reverse) and, similarly, ancillary to her adventures.

CHAPTER 4: GODS AND MONSTERS

The Shifting Mythic Figure of the Doctor

Throughout seasons 25 and 26 we see a marked increase in the use of mythological sources and archetypes in **Doctor Who**. This brings with it a shift away from naturalistic explanations for myth and a move from plot resolutions that depend upon the application of science. David Clark pinpoints the moment of this change to *The Greatest Show in the Galaxy*, in which the Doctor battles the Gods of Ragnarok:

> '[W]hat we have here is not an attempt to debunk mythology, or to provide a rational explanation [...] What we have here is classic **Doctor Who** embracing mythology, accepting that there are beings whom we might well describe as supernatural, who are an integral part of the universe [...] And what's more remarkable is that the story for the first time wants us to believe that the Doctor is one too.'[103]

The Doctor defeats the Gods not through the application of reason, or exposing them as deceitful, but with, in effect a 'magic sword and a magic amulet'[104]. The Gods are dethroned, but they are not debunked.

This mythic turn also brings, as David Rafer has argued, a reconfiguration of the figure of the Doctor: 'The Doctor's mythic identity becomes a particularly dominant theme in the McCoy

---

[103] Clark, David (2016) *Nothing New to Say About Doctor Who 6*, e-book edition, location 1035.
[104] Clark, *Nothing New to Say 6*, e-book edition, location 1035.

era'[105]. Rafer has suggested that the Doctor by this point is suffering from 'a mythic identity crisis'[106], and that aesthetic problems arise in the show from the inclusion of ancient myth:

> 'A tension emerges between science fiction, which generally implies a "logical" narrative based upon the imaginative extrapolation of science, and myth which is more about feelings, intuitions and the unexplained'[107].

This is of course not to say that **Doctor Who** did not use make use of myth and archetypes prior to 1987 (as Rafer points out, examples of the former are numerous). The Doctor has always had elements of the Trickster, the Sage, arguably even the Wandering Jew (an immortal traveller exiled from a lost homeland[108]), and, of course, a touch of the divine in his ability to come back from death. All of this prefigures later archetypal iterations of the Doctor: the Messianic 'Lord of Time' explored in particular in the 2007 series; the 'Oncoming Storm' – a mythic version of the Doctor as 'rebel' and instigator of change referred to by both 10th and 11th incarnations; and the War Doctor – a form of the warrior-priest.

---

[105] Rafer, David, 'Mythic Identity in Doctor Who', in Butler, David, ed. (2007) *Time and Relative Dissertations in Space: Critical perspectives on Doctor Who*, p133.
[106] Rafer, 'Mythic Identity in Doctor Who', p123.
[107] Rafer, 'Mythic Identity in Doctor Who', p130.
[108] Ian Briggs writes:
> 'When I first joined the programme I'd watched the early Hartnell episodes which I'd been too young to watch at the time, with very little biography supplied, and now on *Fenric* that figure came back to me: some kind of eternal traveller with this mysterious time and space conveyance'
> (personal communication with the author, April 2018).

The increased use of myth was partly driven by what has come to be known as the 'Cartmel Master Plan', a fan term for the attempt by Andrew Cartmel to inject mystery into the figure of the Doctor, and, more generally, a darker tone to the character. Ian Briggs remembers:

> 'Andrew was trying to change the Doctor – get rid of accreted biographical baggage which had become a constriction, to free up fresh story possibilities. First time round, on *Dragonfire*, we had nothing to go on for the Doctor's personality apart from Sylvester's two-minute screen test. But by the time of *Fenric* we'd had two seasons of Sylvester's performances to learn from, and the writers were pretty much agreed that taking scenes darker worked well.'[109]

Losing the earlier mythology of the show means that the writers were now able to adapt from other sources more freely, and to experiment with different interpretations of the Doctor's identity. Stephen Wyatt, writer of *Paradise Towers*, recalls:

> 'a conscious junking of the mythology [...] Let's forget about the Master; let's forget about the Time Lords, let's get back to the original idea, which was [that the Doctor was an explorer in] outer space'[110].

Pulling against this were scripts from Ben Aaronovitch and, later, Marc Platt, both of whom extrapolated this new, darker version of the Doctor from established ideas. Some of these later, unmade stories (for example, 'Thin Ice' in which Ace enters the Prydonian

---

[109] Personal communication with the author, April 2018.
[110] Quoted in Howe, Walker, Stammers, *The Handbook Volume Two*, p473

Academy, or, indeed, the whole proposed storyline around Lungbarrow, the Doctor's ancestral House on his homeworld), seem to add at least as much Gallifreyan baggage as they ditch; the point, however, is that the Doctor's identity was under discussion, and the general turn was towards making him powerful on a mythic level. The Doctor participates in the myths used rather than seeking to explicate or demystify them on a rational basis.

Cartmel's description of his own vision makes clear this fundamental shift in the Doctor's mythic identity: '[T]he version I was working towards is like he was this kind of hugely powerful, almost deity-like, godlike kind of being who had existed before the Time Lords'. His instruction to writers was 'write him like he's God'. Perhaps predictably, John Nathan-Turner rapidly squashed this. Cartmel recalls: 'For some reason the notion of Doctor Who as God didn't sit too well with John. He thought there might be some religious repercussions.' Cartmel is clear about the storytelling ramifications. 'That was never what I intended – to make him God. That's not effective, dramatically [...] He's too powerful.'[111] (The 2007 series involves a fuller investigation of what a messianic Doctor might mean that makes liberal use of religious themes, language, and iconography[112].)

In this chapter, I am less concerned with what **Doctor Who** does with myth than with what Rafer identifies as 'the equally intriguing

---

[111] 'Endgame'.

[112] See McCormack, Una, 'He's Not the Messiah: Undermining Political and Religious Authority in New **Doctor Who'**, in Bradshaw, Simon, Antony Keen, and Graham Sleight *The Unsilent Library: Essays on the Russell T. Davies Era of the New Doctor Who* (2011), pp45-62.

problem of what myth does to **Doctor Who**'[113]. I would argue, however, that in *The Curse of Fenric* the tension between myth and science fiction that Rafer identifies is in fact resolved. The story is concerned with the creation of what I would call **secular or humanistic myth**. The Doctor enters an apocalyptic battle – the game of chess – as a player. He does not seek to debunk Fenric – on the contrary, he accepts the full seriousness of the existential threat that Fenric represents – but the means used to defeat Fenric are rational. By this I do not mean that the Doctor resorts to a technical solution. (More importantly, he does not resort to technobabble, which would bring the story firmly into the realm of fantasy.) The resolution is humanist, by which I mean it values human existence and agency, and prefers logical and rational thought to dogma and superstition.

Irrational and uncritical belief is repeatedly interrogated throughout the story: Wainwright cannot sustain his Christianity in the face of the doubts raised by the bombing of German civilians: 'the two-thousand-year-old lie shattered'[114]. Millington plainly believes in the Norse myths, and that Ragnarok is occurring; the novelisation contains an essay purportedly written by him at school, to which a master's comment is appended: 'An extraordinarily vivid piece of writing for a boy of only 12. It is almost as though young Millington really believes that these myths will come true one day.'[115] And, indeed, they do – almost – during the course of the story. No explanation is offered for Fenric beyond the mythic; there's no suggestion, for example, that he is from a powerful 'Elder Race'

---

[113] Rafer, 'Mythic Identity', p128.
[114] Briggs, *The Curse of Fenric*, p153.
[115] Briggs, *The Curse of Fenric*, p43.

spanning the stars whose sufficiently advanced science is indistinguishable from magic (the kind of explanation given, for example, for the Egyptian Gods in *Pyramids of Mars* (1975)). Fenric is exactly what he presents: a powerful and ancient force of Evil.

What are we offered as a resolution to this? Where might we find strength in an age when the old grand narratives are collapsing, and older, less rational superstitions seem to walk the Earth again? Sorin is initially able to hold back the Haemovores by the strength of his belief in the Revolution; in an inspired spin on the traditional vampire story, it is not the symbol that stops the Haemovores, but the belief (Wainwright's cross is defeated). We see Sorin, too, acting as a capable captain, and one who clearly inspires respect and belief from his men. We also know – although we do not see this happen – that Fenric is presumably able to destroy Sorin's faith in the Revolution in order to be able to take over his body. The pawns might unite to defeat the generals, but their victory is not assured. In other words, one should not unthinkingly put faith in that other grand ideological narrative of the 20th century, Communism (hardly unsurprising given the time of writing). But the pawns give us the clue. The crucial moment in *The Curse of Fenric* is when the Doctor holds back the Haemovores not by praying to a god or invoking a cause, but in murmuring his companions' names. Irrationality and superstition, dark and powerful forces, are held back by belief in others: this is how the Tommy and the Comrade survive, through belief in each other rather than in their respective nations or ideologies. The Haemovores are held back by secular and humanist faith. This too, however, is a double-edged sword, and it is in this context that Ace's uncritical faith in the Doctor has to be held to account and reconstructed.

An aside on the Haemovores (or vampires, since vampires they are, despite John Nathan-Turner's refusal to let them be called that): *Dracula* (1897) and *Carmilla* are clear fore-runners, given the setting and the sexualised nature of, in particular, Phyllis and Jean, but another 19th-century antecedent is Karl Marx, who used the vampire as a metaphor for capital[116]: in *Das Kapital*, for instance, Marx describes capital as 'dead labour, that, vampire-like, only lives by sucking living labour, and lives the more, the more labour it sucks.' Elsewhere, Marx describes the stakes of class conflict as 'combat or death: bloody struggle or extinction'[117]. Here the Haemovores are operating on a metaphorical level; the end goal of this exploitation is a dead planet:

DOCTOR

Thousands of years in the future, the Earth lies dying, the surface just a chemical slime. Half a million years of industrial progress.

ANCIENT ONE

I am the last. The last living creature on Earth. I watched my world dying with chemicals, and I could do nothing. My world is dead.

The Curse of Fenric makes free use of mythology and folklore, but the storytelling does not attempt to demythologise or offer naturalistic explanations. Instead, the Doctor enters these stories as a player,

---

[116] Morrissette, Jason J., 'Marxferatu: The Vampire Metaphor as a Tool for Teaching Marx's Critique of Capitalism', in *The Teacher*, July 2013, p637-642.
[117] Morrissette, 'Marxferatu', p639.

taking the existence of gods and monsters at face value, and battling them on these grounds. *The Curse of Fenric* does not refute the mythic nature of archetypal stories, but instead is concerned with destabilising their authority and creating new secular myths and archetypes. These in turn are not religious, or ideological, or even scientific. They are humanist. Religion has failed. Communism has failed too, but personal relationships and collective action may yet offer humanity a chance. We don't see as fully worked through a vision of mythic humanism again until the 2007 season, which also uses a mythic, quasi-religious Doctor to outline a rationally critical understanding of the universe, and assert the power of, in this case, technologically-mediated collective action.

Ursula Le Guin, writing on myth and science fiction, argues that myth is not subordinate to science fiction, and that they are not contradictory[118]:

> 'Myth is one of the several ways the human being, body/psyche, perceives, understands and relates to the world. Like science, it is a product of a basic human mode of apprehension. To pretend that I can be replaced by abstract or quantitative cognition is to assert that the human being is, potentially or ideally, a creature of pure reason [...] We are rational beings, but we are also sensual, emotional, appetitive, ethical beings, driven by needs and reaching out for satisfactions which the intellectual alone cannot provide. Where these other modes of being and doing are inadequate,

---

[118] Le Guin, Ursula K., 'Myth and Archetype in Science Fiction' in *The Language of the Night: essays on fantasy and science fiction* (1989), p61-69.

the intellect should prevail. Where the intellect fails, and must always fail, [...] then one of the other modes must take over. The myth, mythological insight, is one of these. Supremely effective in its area of function, it needs no replacement.'[119]

Science fiction, Le Guin goes on to show, can well make use of myth and archetype (although it doesn't always do so). What science fiction can do with myth is only at least as interesting as what myth can do with science fiction.

What does it mean to write a humanist myth? What could mythic humanism look like? In *The Curse of Fenric*, I believe we come as close to this as **Doctor Who** ever does. The rejection of automatic adherence and belief in grand narratives; the use of reason to reject superstition and dogma; the refusal of obedience to undeserved authority; and the assertion that we have to have (reasonable) faith in each other to survive. In addition, *The Curse of Fenric* is concerned with the uses we make of narrative – grand or otherwise – in our lives, the workings of ideology (and 'curses') and the meaning we can find in the world in the face of the collapse of grand narratives.

In an age where reason no longer wins political arguments, and experts are held in suspicion and contempt, the need for these secular and humanist myths becomes more pressing. Superman fought Nazis; he is a 'submyth', existing '[b]eyond and beneath the great living mythologies of religion and power [...] a region into which science fiction enters'. By submyth, Le Guin means:

'those images, figures and motifs which have no religious resonance and no intellectual or aesthetic value, but which

---

[119] Le Guin, 'Myth and Archetype', p61-62.

are vigorously alive and powerful, so that they cannot be dismissed as mere stereotypes. They are shared by all of us; they are genuinely collective. Superman is a submyth. His father was Nietzsche and his mother was a funnybook, and he is alive and well in the mind of every ten-year-old – and millions of others.'[120]

The Doctor, it seems to me, inhabits precisely this region beyond and beneath our grand narratives of religion and power: his father HG Wells, his mother Auntie Beeb.

What kind of Doctor we need next, and will receive next, is yet to be seen. When I think of the Doctor, I often think of Walter Benjamin's Angel of History:

'There is a painting by Klee called Angelus Novus. An angel is depicted there who looks as though he were about to distance himself from something which he is staring at. His eyes are opened wide, his mouth stands open and his wings are outstretched. The Angel of History must look just so. His face is turned towards the past. Where we see the appearance of a chain of events, he sees one single catastrophe, which unceasingly piles rubble on top of rubble and hurls it before his feet. He would like to pause for a moment, to awaken the dead and to piece together what has been smashed. But a storm is blowing from Paradise, it has caught itself up in his wings and is so strong that the Angel can no longer close them. The storm drives him irresistibly into the future, to which his back is turned, while the rubble-heap before him grows sky-high. That which we call progress,

---

[120] Le Guin, 'Myth and Archetype', p64.

is this storm.'[121]

Pause for a moment, awaken the dead, and piece together what has been smashed. These are acts of memory and repair; acts of healing which honour the past and permit the future. The Doctor is perhaps both the Angel of History, and the Oncoming Storm.

---

[121] Benjamin, Walter, 'Theses on the Philosophy of History' in *Illuminations* (1999), Pimlico, p249.

ACKNOWLEDGEMENTS

Thanks to:

Ian Briggs for taking the time during what was a very busy period to answer a series of questions by email. Thank you, and for your marvellous story.

Simon Guerrier for a well-timed exchange that helped me break the block on Chapter 1, particularly for discussions on the changing context at the BBC, and the relevance of contemporary Conservative social policies.

Philip Purser-Hallard and Paul Simpson for their extreme patience at how late this manuscript was, and who received it with enthusiasm. James Cooray Smith set me thinking during the initial stages of the project. I'm grateful also to Matthew Kilburn for help during the final stages, particularly cheering me on.

I am extremely grateful to people who at various points helped me source relevant information: Mark Wright, Cavan Scott, Andrew and Julie Pixley, James Tomlinson, and Stuart Ian Burns. My very grateful thanks to you all.

BIBLIOGRAPHY

Books

Aldred, Sophie, and Tucker, Mike, *Ace! The Inside Story of the End of An Era*. London, Virgin Publishing Ltd, 1996. ISBN 9781852275747.

Ang, Ien, *Watching Dallas: Soap Opera and the Melodramatic Imagination*. London, Routledge, 1985. ISBN 9780415045988.

Benjamin, Walter. *Illuminations*. London, Pimlico, 1999. ISBN 9780712665759.

Bradshaw, Simon, Keen, Antony, and Sleight, Graham, eds, *The Unsilent Library: Essays on the Russell T. Davies Era of the New Doctor Who*. London, The Science Fiction Foundation, 2011. ISBN 9780903007085.

Briggs, Ian, *Doctor Who: The Curse of Fenric*. **The Target Doctor Who Library** #151. London, WH Allen, 1990. ISBN 9780426203483.

Brunsdon, Charlotte, *The Feminist, the Housewife and the Soap Opera*. Oxford, Clarendon Press, 2000. ISBN 9780198159810.

Butler, David, ed, *Time and Relative Dissertations in Space: Critical Perspectives on Doctor Who*. Manchester, Manchester University Press, 2007. ISBN 9780719076824.

Cartmel, Andrew, *Script Doctor: The Inside Story of Doctor Who 1986-89*. London, Reynolds and Hearn Ltd, 2005. ISBN 9781903111895.

Cartmel, Andrew. *Atom Bomb Blues*. **Doctor Who: The Past Doctor Adventures**. London, BBC Books, 2005. ISBN 9780563486350.

Clark, David (2016) *Nothing New to Say about Doctor Who 6*, e-book edition. ASIN B018MZEGIQ.

Cooray Smith, James. *The Massacre*. **The Black Archive** #2. Edinburgh, Obverse Books, 2016. ISBN 9781909031388.

Cornell, Paul, *Love and War*. **Doctor Who: The New Adventures**, London, Virgin Publishing Ltd, 1992. ISBN 9780426203858.

Cornell, Paul, Martin Day and Keith Topping, *The Doctor Who Discontinuity* Guide, London, Virgin Publishing, 1995. ISBN 9780426204428

Davies, William, ed *Economic Science Fictions*. London, Goldsmiths Press, 2017. ISBN 0791906897680.

DeCandido, Keith RA, ed *Doctor Who Short Trips: The Quality of Leadership*. Maidenhead, Big Finish Productions, 2007. ISBN 9781844352692.

Dicks, Terrance, *Timewyrm: Exodus*. **Doctor Who: The New Adventures**. London, Virgin Publishing Ltd, 1991. ISBN 9780426203575.

Ellison, Harlan, ed *Again, Dangerous Visions*. New York, Signet, 1972. ISBN 9780385079532.

Fukuyama, Francis. *The End of History and the Last Man*. New York, Free Press, 1992. ISBN 9780029109752.

Hare, David, *Plenty*. London, Faber, 2000. ISBN 9780571112395.

Heinlein, Robert A., *Starship Troopers*. London, Hodder, 2015. ISBN 9781473616110.

Howe, David, Walker, Stephen James, and Stammers, Mark, ed *The Handbook: The Unofficial and Unauthorised Guide to the Production of Doctor Who, Volume Two*, Bromley, Telos Publishing, 2016. ISBN 9781845839420.

Lane, Andy and Jim Mortimore, *Lucifer Rising*. **Doctor Who: The New Adventures**. London, Virgin Publishing Ltd, 1993. ISBN 9780426203889.

Le Fanu, Joseph Sheridan, *Carmilla*. Toronto, House of Pomegrantes Press, 2012. ISBN 9780978454357.

Le Guin, Ursula K. *The Language of the Night: essays on fantasy and science fiction*. London, The Women's Press, 1989. ISBN 9780704342026.

Le Guin, Ursula K. *The Left Hand of Darkness*. London, Orbit, 1989. ISBN 9781841496061.

Le Guin, Ursula K. *Steering the Craft: Exercises and Discussions on Story Writing for the Lone Mariner and the Mutinous Crew*. Portland, The Eighth Mountain Press, 1998. ISBN 9780933377462.

Leonard, Paul. *The Turing Test*. **Doctor Who: Eighth Doctor Adventures**. London, BBC Books, 2000. ISBN 9780563538066.

Marson, Richard. *JN-T: The Life and Scandalous Times of John Nathan-Turner*. Tadworth, Miwk Publishing, 2013. ISBN 9781908630131.

McIntee, David A., *Autumn Mist*. **Doctor Who: Eighth Doctor Adventures**. London, BBC Books, 1999. ISBN 9780563555834.

Parkin, Lance, *Just War*. **Doctor Who: The New Adventures**. London, Virgin Publishing Ltd, 1996. ISBN 9780426204633.

Russ, Joanna, *The Country You Have Never Seen: Essays and Reviews*. Liverpool, Liverpool University Press, 2005. ISBN 9780853238591.

Russ, Joanna, *The Female Man*. London, The Women's Press, 1985. ISBN 9780704347373.

Russ, Joanna, *How To Suppress Women's Writing*. London, The Women's Press, 1984. ISBN 9781477316252.

Russ, Joanna, *The Two of Them*. London, The Women's Press, 1986. ISBN 9780819567604.

Russ, Joanna, *To Write Like a Woman: Essays in Feminism and Science Fiction*. Bloomington, Indiana University Press, 1995. ISBN 9780253209832.

Scott, Cavan, and Mark Wright, eds, *Doctor Who Short Trips: The Ghosts of Christmas*. Maidenhead, Big Finish Productions, 2007. ISBN 9781844352708.

Matthewman, Scott, 'Tell Me You Love Me'.

Stanish, Deborah, and LM Myles, eds *Chicks Unravel Time: Women Journey Through Every Season of Doctor Who*. Des Moines, Iowa, Mad Norwegian Press, 2012. ISBN 9781835234128.

Tucker, Mike and Robert Perry, *Illegal Alien*. **Doctor Who: The Monster Collection**. London, BBC Books, 2014. ISBN 9781849907576.

Wood, Tat, *1985-1989: Seasons 22-26, The TV Movie*. **About Time 6: The Unauthorized Guide to Doctor Who** #6,Des Moines, Iowa, Mad Norwegian Press, 2007. ISBN 9780975944653.

Periodicals

Fukuyama, Francis, 'The End of History?' *The National Interest* #16, Summer 1989.

Moore, Alan and Ian Gibson, 'The Ballad of Halo Jones' *2000 AD* Prog 376, 7 July 1984.

Television

'Allo, 'Allo. BBC, 1982-1992.

The Bletchley Circle. ITV, 2012-.

Blue Remembered Hills. BBC, 1979.

Carrie's War. BBC, 1974.

Colditz. BBC, 1972-74.

Coronation Street. Granada for ITV, 1960-

Dad's Army. BBC, 1968-77.

The Diary of Anne Frank. BBC, 1987.

Doctor Who. BBC, 1963-.

> *Survival*, 1989. DVD release, 2007.

> > 'Endgame'. DVD extra.

> > 'Little Girl Lost'. DVD extra.

Enemy at the Door. LWT for ITV, 1978-80.

Fortunes of War. BBC/WGBH (Boston)/Primetime Television for BBC, 1987.

Foyle's War. ITV, 2002-2015.

Goodnight, Sweetheart. BBC, 1993-99.

How We Used to Live. BBC, 1968-2002.

The Imitation Game. BBC, 1980.

It Ain't Half Hot, Mum. BBC, 1974-81.

The Sarah Jane Adventures. BBC, 2007-2011.

    Lost in Time (2010).

Secret Army. BBC, 1977-79.

Spitting Image. ITV.

Tenko. BBC, 1981-84.

Torchwood. BBC, 2006-2011.

    Captain Jack Harkness (2007).

The Winds of War. Paramount Television for ABC, 1983.

Wish Me Luck. ITV, 1988-90.

Film

Brooks, Mel, dir, *The Producers*. Embassy Pictures, 1967.

Gilbert, Lewis, dir, *Operation Daybreak*. American Allied Features, 1975.

Hamilton, Guy, dir, *The Colditz Story*. Ivan Foxwell Productions, 1955.

Hutton, Brian G., dir, *Where Eagles Dare*. Gershwin-Kastner Productions, 1968.

Mann, Anthony, dir, *The Heroes of Telemark*. Benton Film Productions, 1965.

Tyldum, Morten, dir, *The Imitation Game*. Black Bear Pictures, 2014.

Audio CD

Barnes, Alan, *The Girl Who Never Was*. Big Finish Productions, 2007.

Fitton, Matt, *A Life of Crime*. Big Finish Productions, 2016.

Foley, Tim, **Gallifrey: Time War**: *Soldier Obscura*, Big Finish Productions, 2018.

Handcock, Scott and David Llewellyn, **Gallifrey**: *Intervention Earth*, Big Finish Productions, 2015.

Lyons, Steve, *Colditz*. Big Finish Productions, 2001.

McCormack, Una, 'An Eye for Murder'. *Breaking Bubbles and Other Stories*. Big Finish Productions, 2014.

Mulryne, Phil, Alan Barnes, Justin Richards and Ken Bentley. **The Churchill Years** #1. Big Finish Productions, 2016.

Oliver, Mark B, 'Dark Convoy'. *Doctor Who: Short Trips 5*. Big Finish Productions, 2015 (download only).

Potter, Ian, *The Alchemists*. **The Companion Chronicles** #8. Big Finish Productions, 2013.

Platt, Marc, *Thin Ice*. **Doctor Who: The Lost Stories**. Big Finish Productions, 2011.

Web

Adams, Stephen, 'Doctor Who "Had Anti-Thatcher Agenda"'. The *Telegraph*, 14 February 2010. https://www.telegraph.co.uk/culture/tvandradio/doctor-who/7235547/Doctor-Who-had-anti-Thatcher-agenda.html. Accessed 9 July 2018.

Angelini, Sergio, 'WWII Dramas'. BFI screenonline. www.screenonline.org.uk/tv/id/1127960/. Accessed 9 July 2018.

Leapman, Michael, 'Alasdair Milne: BBC Executive who Rose to Director-General But Was Sacked Under Pressure from Mrs Thatcher'. The *Independent*, 10 January 2006.

https://www.independent.co.uk/news/obituaries/alasdair-milne-bbc-executive-who-rose-to-director-general-but-was-sacked-under-pressure-from-mrs-8446767.html. Accessed 9 July 2018.

Morrissette, Jason J., 'Marxferatu: The Vampire Metaphor as a Tool for Teaching Marx's Critique of Capitalism'. The Teacher, July 2013. https://www.cambridge.org/core/services/aop-cambridge-core/content/view/1990E750B8DE51FF7B173F6B12F9C1A3/S1049 096513000607a.pdf/div-class-title-marxferatu-the-vampire-metaphor-as-a-tool-for-teaching-marxandapos-s-critique-of-capitalism-div.pdf. Accessed 6 July 2018.

Plunkett, John, 'BBC Puts an End to Producer Choice'. The *Guardian*, 22 March 2006. https://www.theguardian.com/media/2006/mar/22/bbc.broadcasti ng. Accessed 9 July 2018.

Tarry, James, '*Doctor Who* Episodes and Spin-offs That Never Happened.' Den of Geek, June 2011. http://www.denofgeek.com/tv/doctor-who/20863/doctor-who-episodes-and-spin-offs-that-never-happened. Accessed 9 July 2018.

BIOGRAPHY

Una McCormack is a *New York Times* bestselling science fiction writer. She has written a handful of **Doctor Who** novels, as well as **Doctor Who** audio dramas, short stories, journalism, and essays. She also writes novels based on **Star Trek: Deep Space 9** and **Star Trek: Discovery**. She has a doctorate in sociology and teaches creative writing at a university. She is a regular broadcaster and podcaster, and, in 2017, was a judge for the Arthur C Clarke Award, given yearly for the best science fiction novel published in the UK. She lives in Cambridge with her partner, daughter and their Dalek. Her favourite television programme is **Blake's 7**.

Coming Soon